The Life of Rex

Rex Makemson

Dedication

I'd like to dedicate the book, of course, to my dearest companions, Misty and Charlie. If there is a Heaven, they will definitely be there.

But perhaps I should also give thought to my ex-wife, Antoinette. If she hadn't left, none of this would have happened. So, thank you, Antoinette – you deserve a mention.

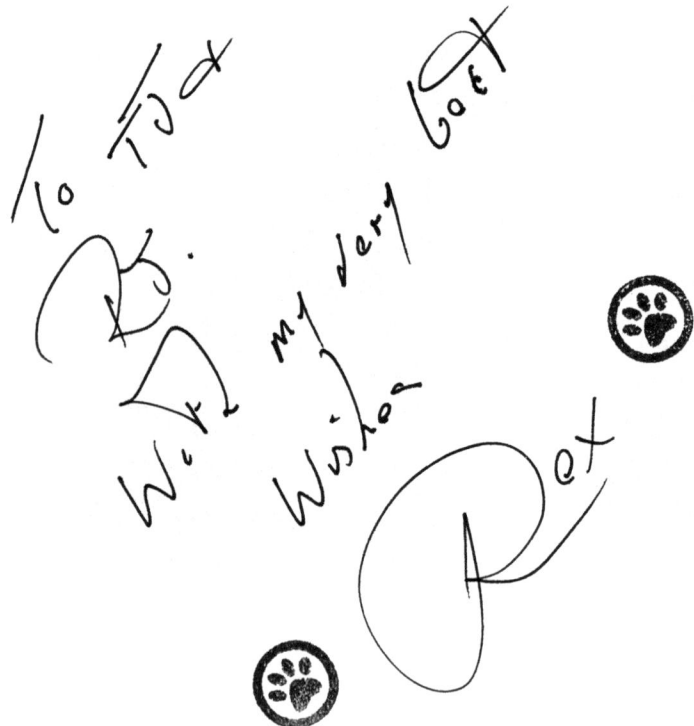

Acknowledgement

The Kennel Club

The British Institute of Professional Dog Trainers

Pets As Therapy UK

About the Author

I'm getting on a bit now and didn't start training dogs until around 2002. My wife left, and I was alone with Misty. I decided to take her to a local training school, which ultimately turned out to be more about bully training than anything else, something I didn't like. In the end, I thought I could do better, so I sorted out the British Institute of Professional Dog Trainers and enrolled in their courses. I started a training school called Paws Obedience Training in Dersingham, Norfolk, England, and also trained at other local village halls, such as those in Rudham and Hunstanton, both in Norfolk. And that's where the story begins.

Contents

Dedication i
Acknowledgement ii
About the Author iii
Introduction 1
Chapter 1 3
Chapter 2 12
Chapter 3 20
Chapter 4 34
Chapter 5 47
Chapter 6 66
Chapter 7 79
Chapter 8 90
Chapter 9 106
Chapter 10 123
Chapter 11 138
Chapter 12 157
Chapter 13 171
Chapter 14 187
Chapter 15 203

Introduction

To explain the relationship between the storyteller and the story: My name is Rex, and I have had two amazing dogs named Misty and Charlie. Misty was a Gold Kennel Club-tested dog who later became a therapy dog. She was also my stooge dog—a dog I could rely on as a behaviourist to ignore aggression from other dogs and help calm them down.

Charlie, on the other hand, was a clever trick dog who thrived on learning new routines. He even made up his own dance routines changing what I taught him and improving on it. He loved performing in these routines and brought joy to schools and public events, where he demonstrated his prowess. I am now the dog, Misty is transformed into Missy, a human, and Charlie also appears as a human character named Charlie. Although the roles have changed, the story is rooted in real experiences from my 20+ years as a dog trainer and behaviourist.

These experiences with Misty and Charlie have been the best of my life. I hope you enjoy reading them as much as I enjoyed living them.

Chapter 1

The Life of Rex

I'm going to slip back—not in time (not yet, anyway)—but into the mind of my namesake, 'Rex.' By Rex, I mean all dogs, big or small, male or female, from every breed you can imagine. Together, we'll look at the world through a puppy's eyes, experiencing life for the first time. Imagine being born, smelling the world before you can see it, then opening your eyes, meeting your siblings, and becoming a human's companion. And oh, the strange things I'd have to learn—like the mysterious language these towering creatures use and the odd things they do with their front paws! But I won't spoil all the surprises.

Hello to a very cute little puppy (I have to say that). The breed doesn't matter. I'm one of many puppies, though I can't count, so I don't know how many. It feels like more than just me. Everything is warm and damp, and something rough keeps wiping over me. I fumble around, bumping into soft, furry bundles—my siblings. I can smell something that makes me hungry, a warm and comforting scent. I wiggle and nudge my way toward it until I find what I'm looking for: food! It fills me with warmth and comfort, and I use my nose to remember where to find it next time. My siblings? Well, they're in the way, but I've learned to push them aside when needed.

Once, while I was drinking, one of my siblings started sucking on my ear! I used my bum to push them away. No way was I letting them stretch my ears out of shape (not that I knew that at the time).

Then something odd happened—suddenly, I could see! Bright light filled the space, and I blinked, taking it all in. There were more animals around me, much like me, though I didn't understand that yet. My siblings, once just warm shapes, were now visible little bundles of fur like me, all crawling and playing. We still pushed each other, still fought for the same food, but now I could see where it came from—our mother. She was huge! Much bigger than us, and it was her tongue that kept wiping us down. I had to admit, it felt kind of nice.

Life was a simple routine: crawl, play, sleep. What more could a puppy want? I thought this was all there was to life until, suddenly, something new happened. A massive creature appeared. This one stood on two legs, which seemed strange. I later learned these were called humans, but back then, they just looked odd. They had long toes on their front paws that wiggled around on their own, holding things and making them move.

One of these humans did something unexpected—it changed our food! Instead of feeding from our mother, we got warm, lumpy stuff in something hard and round (I later learned it's called a bowl). We dove in, faces first, battling for space like always—feet in, bums in, food flying everywhere. We even licked it off each other. What a mess! Afterwards, the humans cleaned us off with something warm and damp—definitely not our mother tongue, but close enough.

As we grew, sharp things started to appear in our mouths—teeth! They were perfect for chomping on food, but not so great during playtime. A few of my siblings got too rough, and I'd bite back when they bit too hard. We also discovered odd noises from our tummies, followed by strange smells from our rear ends. The first time it happened, I was startled! I thought noises only came from the mouth. But no, apparently, there were two ways to make noise and smell. My siblings seemed just as surprised, and we quickly learned to move away from whoever was responsible for the stinkiest surprises.

One little problem arose for us, but it seemed like a big one for our caring human. It happened during what I called the "dark time"—when the humans blocked out all the lights and left. We still wanted food, but our mother wasn't feeding us anymore. We had these sharp things in our mouths now, and feeding hurt her. So, the human took over, bringing us warm, lumpy food in a bowl. We missed the soft feeding from our mother, but the bowl food was good.

During the dark time, things got messy. We didn't go outside to get rid of our water—or anything else—so we did it right where we lived. When the human came to feed us, we'd get excited, jumping and tumbling around. This made a real mess! Our water, and other stuff, got all over us. The human would make a funny sound like "Arrrrgh!" every time this happened, then clean us up and our living space. But we hated waiting—food was coming, and we weren't about to be patient!

Many sleeps later, we were picked up and taken to a place with odd smells and strange noises. Other animals were there, making all sorts of sounds, and one made a high-pitched "meee-ow." A human picked me up, checking my mouth, ears, and even my tummy (how rude!). Suddenly, I felt a sharp sting near the back of my neck. It hurt, and I said, "Ow!" though it didn't sound quite the same as that other animal. I hadn't done anything wrong, so why was I hurt?

Thankfully, once we were outside, the fresh air felt better. There were small humans—little versions of the big ones—waiting to cuddle us. They made funny noises and kept pressing their mouths to our heads, making slurping sounds. I wondered—were they trying to suck us up like food? For a moment, I worried I might be swallowed whole!

Back home, I noticed something strange. Our big furry mother was free to go anywhere, but we were kept in a small area and only taken out for short breaks. At first, they put us on crinkly stuff under our feet, which confused me. We'd always gone wherever we were, and our mother would clean it up. Now it was different.

One time, while on the crinkly stuff, I squatted, and something smelly came out. One of my litter mates sniffed it, then tried to lick it! They quickly rolled away in disgust. I doubt they'll try that again.

We spent a lot of time playing and, well, biting. My mouth was getting sore with these new sharp teeth. Biting things helped relieve the soreness, so naturally, we all started biting and pulling on each other. It didn't take long for us to learn that biting too hard hurt.

Then, we were finally allowed to go outside! Well, sort of. At first, it felt strange, but soon I realised it was great fun. We'd roll and jump around on soft, green stuff that felt good under my paws. The human-made noises while we played, saying things that sounded like "Blah blah whee blah wee." I didn't know what they were saying, but I didn't care. This big open space felt amazing!

After playtime, when my tummy started aching, I let out water right there on the soft stuff. Back inside, the human kept saying something like "Bood Booy" and seemed happy. I got food and strokes on my back, which felt so good I nearly went again right there!

Over time, many big and small humans came to see us. They'd pick us up, make "Ahhh" sounds, and hold us close. But one day, after a visit, one of my littermates was picked up—and didn't come back. I didn't understand. We'd been getting on well, so why had they disappeared?

After that, I got nervous whenever visitors came. I didn't want to be next, so I tried being extra nice. But soon, I found myself in a cage, trapped inside while a human looked in. What had I done wrong? I just wanted my mother and siblings. I didn't mean to upset anyone—I was only trying to be nice.

Then things got even weirder. I could hear strange noises—smells I'd never smelt before filled the air, and there was a loud droning sound that went up and down. I was being bounced around in the cage, slipping on the floor, and I felt scared. At one point, the door opened, and I tumbled backwards. A big face looked in at me, but then I heard a loud, quick noise: "Wose ert!" The door slammed shut again.

I could hear what sounded like squeaky humans. Their voices were all different, and I didn't understand any of them. One voice was louder, making sharp noises like "Beeee qwyart!" Another voice, higher-pitched, sounded softer and a little more comforting. It made a sound like, "Ssshhhh, bee moan soon." It felt almost soothing, but still, I was confused. I had no idea what they were saying, and all the bouncing and strange smells were making me shake. I cried a little more. Where was Mum? Where were all the others? Why was this happening?

I was so lonely. I let out some water—and some of the other smelly stuff—because I couldn't hold it in anymore. And because I kept bouncing around, I got a bit covered in it all. The smells, combined with everything else, were awful. What's going to happen to me? I'm so sorry if I did something wrong.

Chapter 2

The New Home

The noises outside the box were confusing. I could hear grating sounds, similar to when humans walked over the hard, round things surrounding the place where we played on the soft, wet stuff. Could I be back there? But no, this felt different. The noise stopped, and I felt like I was being moved somewhere. I could still smell the small humans nearby, one scent stronger than the other. Suddenly—Bang! Bang! Bang!—loud noises echoed all around me, and I jolted with each one. The last bang was even closer. I was frightened but unhurt, hoping they wouldn't sting me like they did in that smelly place before.

The carrier I was in opened, and I blinked, looking around. This was definitely a new place; everything looked strange, with unfamiliar colours and very sweet smells that were almost too strong. A small human with a higher voice picked me up, stroking me. It felt nice, but I was still nervous. They kept making "Aargh" noises, but I couldn't figure out why.

After a while, they put me down in a small area with a soft, lumpy mass in one corner. It smelled a bit strange. How do humans put up with such sweet smells? I wanted to find my Mum and siblings, but there was no way out. I jumped at the barrier, but it didn't move. The space was empty—just me, a lumpy spot, a water bowl (which I hoped held only water), and some big humans watching me from above. They were so tall, making me feel small and confused.

I was scared but curious and thirsty, too, so I went to the bowl. The water was surprisingly good—cold and refreshing. Feeling a bit better, I looked around for food. I hadn't eaten in a long time, and my belly was growling. I hoped it wouldn't be much longer.

Then I heard something, "Shmelly Poopy." The big human with the gentler voice picked me up and rubbed me with something wet and rough—not their tongue like my Mum, but from their front paws. I didn't like it. I was getting used to my smell! It wasn't that bad, but humans seemed to prefer different smells than I did. Once they finished, I was back in the small area. I sniffed around, still hoping to find my Mum or my siblings. Empty. No one was here except me.

Lonely, I curled up on a small piece of soft stuff that smelled faintly like Mum. Comforted, I began to fall asleep but was startled awake when a big human placed a food bowl in front of me. The smell was familiar, and I ate it all quickly. It wasn't much, but it was better than nothing. I let out a little tummy water, then curled up with the piece that smelled like Mum and drifted into a deep sleep.

I dreamed of Mum and the silly fights with my siblings. But when I woke, everything was dark. I wandered around, but I couldn't get out of the small area. There were walls all around, and I could see through them, but there was no way out. Had I been moved while I slept? I didn't know when or how.

The darkness made everything worse. I felt so lonely and began to cry, calling out in hopes that the humans were still nearby. What if I was here all alone, forever?

Suddenly, it got bright again, and I saw a big human rubbing their eyes. Before I knew it, I was being picked up, still a bit wet from knocking over my water bowl earlier. The human carried me outside to the soft, wet stuff. It was very dark, but I could see okay. The human stumbled and opened their mouth wide, making "Aargh" noises. My tummy ached, so I let out some tummy water. The human went a bit silly, repeating "bood booy" over and over. I didn't know what it meant, but I felt a bit less lonely.

Not long after, I was back in my comfort area with a small meal waiting for me. The little, squeaky human had left the thing they'd been carrying, so I pawed at it, then bit it, hoping it would make a sound. It didn't, but it helped with my mouth soreness. I was having fun biting and shaking it until, suddenly, it fell apart! Bits of it were everywhere, but it had been so soothing.

Then the small human returned and saw what I'd done. A loud noise burst from their mouth, "Eeargh!" Their eyes started leaking water, and they shouted, "Ummy! Ummy!" The big human arrived quickly and made noises to calm the small human, who ran off, still yelping. I didn't know what was going on—this was all so confusing. I wish I understood what they were saying.

The big human cleaned up the bits of the thing I'd chewed up. In its place, they gave me a large, cold, wet rod. I put it in my mouth, and it felt strange—very cold, but it soothed my aching gums. I played with it for ages, and it kept getting wetter as I chewed. It was almost like the water I drank from the bowl, but much colder.

<u>Rex's Thoughts</u> - *This cold thing is quite hard and looks like lots of stuff wound together with big lumpy bits at each end, a good thought by the hoomans it helps a lot.*

Settling In

The small human with a better bark than the other little one came in and picked me up. They had my chew toy and put me down in the very big open area where the humans like to sit. We started playing pull games with the toy. It was great fun! I thought humans would be stronger, but I kept winning—well, most of the time. Once, the small human picked up the chew toy with me hanging onto the end. I was a long way off the ground! I didn't want to let go in case I fell, but eventually, I was put down. It was fun, really.

I think I'm going to have to figure out what to call these humans so you know who I'm talking about. I'll listen carefully to what they call each other and try to work it out.

Still, I don't understand why I'm on my own. I miss my siblings and my birth mother. It feels strange without them.

Outside, it was getting darker. The inside bright things had been turned on, and the see-through bits in the walls were much darker than before. I figured I had more food coming soon.

What a great guess! The large human with the high voice came with more food. This human smells very odd, kind of sweet, and it makes me cough a bit. I got a few bowls of food, which is great because I'm getting bigger now.

Playing chew games with the humans is fun, but their noises are a bit annoying when I accidentally grab their hands with my mouth. The little squeaky human hasn't come near me since I chewed up her plaything, which I thought was left for me. I'm not sure what the upset is about.

After I finished eating, I was picked up and taken outside again. Why do they keep doing this just after I eat? It's nice outside, but they always shout the same sound— "oylet, oylet." I think they said that last time I let my tummy water out. I'll try it again and see what happens. Ahh, what a relief! And sure enough, the big human started shouting "bood booy, bood booy" again. I think that sound means they're pleased. I'm getting good at this, I hope.

Chapter 3

Routine and Surprises

The routine went on like this for a few more big light changes. I ate plenty of food, went outside after each bowl, and sometimes heard the good sounds—"bood booy." Occasionally, I had to go in my comfort area, but no one barked at me, even when the squeaky human cried the other day. I also had lots of playtime with the tall, sweet-smelling human and the small human who played with me before. We had fun, except when they yelped as I put my mouth on their hands.

They still gave me the cold, wet chew toy that helped my sore mouth. I don't know why my mouth hurts so much, but the toy really helps when I bite it.

One day, after my second meal, the squeaky human came back and picked me up. She started rubbing my back with her hand, and I have to admit, it felt nice. I let her do it for a little while, but then I got bored and wanted to play. I tried to jump to the ground, but I fell over (I'm not very good at that yet). She grabbed my wet chew toy and flashed it in front of me. I grabbed it, and we had the same tugging game I played with the other little human. They're clever with how they use their front paws! I'm glad this one is playing with me now.

Rex's Thoughts – *I can't help thinking how odd hoomans are walking upright must be really hard and there good at it and the long things they have on their front paws really good for holding things.*

Meeting a Big Dog

After a few more big light changes, even more humans came into the enclosure. At first, it was fun because they all wanted to play with me. Then, I noticed something—a creature like me, but as big as my birth mother! It had a different-looking coat and didn't seem interested in playing. I backed away, scared, and tried to hide behind the squeaky human.

The big creature followed me. One of the humans picked me up, but the big thing jumped up, trying to reach me! All the humans started barking at once. Then I heard "bood booy" again and again, and the big human pushed me toward the creature. I was terrified! The big creature sniffed me all over, and I was sure I'd be eaten. Its mouth was huge! But after all that sniffing, nothing bad happened, and I was put back in my comfort area.

I was exhausted but couldn't settle. I kept looking at the big thing and all the humans watching me. Even though I was really scared, maybe it wasn't as bad as I thought it would be.

The Vet and New Discoveries

We went through another big light change a couple more times. Besides one accident during the dark time, everything stayed the same. Then something different happened. The big, deep-voiced human picked me up, and the other big one with the high voice came along too. I'll have to come up with easier names for them soon.

They took me to the thing that brought me here from my siblings. I didn't like this. After lots of bangs and roaring, we ended up at a place with a familiar smell—and I did not like it. I remembered the last time I was here. I got stung in the back.

Sure enough, the same human came out and waved their front paw. We went into a small area, just like last time. I was stroked and prodded, and they looked in my eyes, ears, and even opened my mouth. It was all very uncomfortable.

Then—I GOT STUNG AGAIN. It hurt! I tried to bite the hand that stung me, but I missed and accidentally bit the big human on their toe. They yelped but didn't do anything, except bark at the other human who'd stung me.

After that, I got some little bits of food. The tall, high-barking human called it "shweety." I'd heard that word before. I think it's what they give me when they say "bood booy" and pet me.

We went back to my safe place. I was taken outside, and I let my water out. Then I let out the other stuff. Once again, I heard "bood booy" and got lots of strokes. Later, I played with the small human who normally plays with me, and I quickly forgot the sting.

The Collar

Then something strange happened. They put something around my neck. This had happened a few times before, but they'd always taken it off quickly, so I didn't think much of it. But this time, it stayed on.

At first, I didn't mind too much, but it felt strange. I tried to claw it off, but it didn't work. Eventually, I gave up. When I stopped, the humans gave me "shweety" food, which was nice. Then they took it off again.

More light changes. More play. They kept putting the thing around my neck, and I figured it out! If I leave it on, I get more "shweety" food. I'm fooling these humans, really.

I've also figured out that if I go outside to get rid of my water, I get "shweety" food too. Easy stuff! Piece of cake, this life.

Figuring Out Names

I think I've figured out what the humans call each other.

The big human with the loud bark is "Daard." The big human with the higher bark is "Moom." The small human with the very squeaky voice is "Missy," and the other small human who plays with me a lot is "Shaarly."

I think I've got it right.

The Cold Chew Toy

They keep giving me the cold, wet toy, which I like. My mouth still hurts a lot. Something's wrong in there—it aches and hurts at the same time.

But chewing the cold toy helps. I play with it for ages. It's wet, like the water I drink, but colder. It soothes the soreness in my mouth, and I'm starting to feel better about it.

You should know a little about Rex's teeth. He started with none, but then his 28 baby teeth came in. Now that he's growing, he's beginning to develop his 42 permanent teeth—20 on top and 22 on the bottom. That's why he chews so much! It helps soothe the ache as his teeth and mouth grow.

Understanding How Dogs Think

Before we return to Rex's adventures, this is probably a good time to step out of his world for a moment and explain how a dog's mind works when trying to understand humans.

Dogs don't hear words the way we do. They don't know what the alphabet is, and they don't understand vowels or consonants. To a dog, the words we say are just noises—sounds they have to interpret. And this is where dogs become very clever. They have to figure out what each sound means, often by relying on more than just the sound itself.

The first thing dogs look at is your body language because that's how they communicate with each other. Dogs use posture, the position of their heads, the movement of their ears, and other physical cues to express themselves. So when you talk to a dog, they aren't just listening to the sound of your voice—they're watching your every move.

Now, think about how smart a dog has to be to understand us. How do they know when we're happy with them or annoyed? For example, remember earlier when Rex was called a "good boy"? To him, that phrase is just a sound. What mattered most was the tone of voice used. It was calm and reassuring, which told Rex he had done something right.

You might also notice that when Rex had accidents or tore up the toy, he wasn't scolded. Instead, the girl was told off a bit by her dad for leaving the toy out. If you make it hard for a dog to distinguish between "good boy" and "bad boy," things get confusing. If a dog does something wrong and there's no reaction from you, they might try harder to get your attention—even by doing things you don't want—because they're used to getting some kind of response.

Of course, this is a simplified explanation, but you can see how important tone, body language, and consistency are when communicating with dogs.

As for Rex's family, we now know them as the Richardsons: Mum, Dad, 8-year-old daughter Missy, and 10-year-old Charlie.

Now, let's return to the joys of puppyhood with Rex.

More Changes and New Discoveries

Something serious just happened. One of my hard, sharp bits—my tooth!—came out while I was chewing on my cold toy. I noticed it stuck there a few light changes ago, and I think I even saw it on the floor at one point. This is very serious! What if I lose all my teeth? How will I chew or play properly ever again? Especially now that my food is changing—it's not as soft as it used to be. Some of it has hard bits, and I really enjoy chewing those.

All the humans in the house seem really excited about something. I know it has to do with me because they keep making noises and pointing at me. Missy keeps putting a long piece of something onto my collar, which stops me from going too far. It feels a bit unfair, but it's fun to chew on when I get the chance! Missy gets a bit annoyed when I start chewing it, though, and takes it off. I think it's a plaything, but she probably doesn't want me running away with it.

Another big light change has passed. I've been sleeping more and waking up less during the dark time. But I'm still up before all the humans, and sometimes I bark when I need to let my water out. Usually, Moomy is the one who lets me out. She always gives me an extra shweety after I go, and sometimes I even get to run around outside for a bit—unless there's a lot of water falling from the sky. I don't like that much.

Training Starts

I'm allowed to roam the bigger areas now! I only go back to the comfort area when they want me to sleep, but sometimes I doze off in other spots around the house. No one seems to mind or move me. I like that because it means I can explore a lot. Although, when I explore with my mouth, they hand me the cold chew toy again. So, I fool them as usual—if I feel like having the cold toy, I just nibble on their skin coverings. Why don't they have fur like me? Then they wouldn't need all these things hanging off them!

Something is happening. Moom, Missy, and Shaarly are putting on extra skin coverings, and Missy is holding the long neck connector. I'm being picked up, which must mean we're going outside!

We're getting into the big noisy box again, the one I was in before. But this time, I'm allowed to move around! Missy has me on her lap and is holding onto the neck connector so I can't go too far. This is a bit strange. We're moving now, all together, sitting in this box. Moomy is holding onto something at the front, and when she moves it, the big box moves too. We went backwards first, then forwards, and now we're going faster—faster than I could ever run! It's so strange. I'm sitting on Missy's legs, and I'm not even getting tired!

I feel a bit unsure about where we're going, but Missy and Shaarly seem excited, making lots of noise together. Moomy says "shooosh," and they stop. I don't know what that bark means, but we've slowed down now.

The big box stops, and we're in a place with lots of other big boxes lined up.

We stopped next to one with a dog like me inside. It's about my size, maybe a little fatter, with funny markings and a very squished nose! It's looking at me in a strange way but isn't shouting. I wonder where we're going. This isn't the place where I got stung... is it?

I'm being put down, and the line has been attached to my neck band so I can't wander too far. I see a few other puppies like me — different shapes, sizes, and colours — all on long lines next to their big boxes. Missy seems very excited, making noises at all the other little dogs around us. I hope she doesn't like them more than me!

This is starting to feel like it's going to be great playday, as long as the other dogs are friendly. I hope they are.

We're all moving now, and I'm pulling as hard as I can to get inside the big building with all these baby dogs.

I want to play! But I keep getting pulled back. Daard is holding me, keeping me from going too fast. He's not stopping me completely, just letting some other puppies go in first. Finally, it's my turn!

Inside, we all stand around, looking at each other. Some of the other puppies are shouting, but I stay quiet. I'm a bit nervous but also excited. I think I've seen this place before... and that voice out front... It sounds familiar.

The smell! It's the same as the place where I got stung. TWICE. Oh no... This isn't good.

Chapter 4

First Puppy Socialisation Day

Why are all these puppies so happy to be here? I got *stung* the last time I saw this big hooman. He's not nice. Now he's sitting on the floor, making noises to all the hoomans. What's going on?

Missy picks me up, and I see all the other hoomans picking up their puppies, too. We're being moved to a place that looks a lot like the one I get put in at home—only much bigger. Are we all going to be hurt at the same time? I start shouting to warn everyone, and some of the other puppies do the same.

Missy puts me down inside the big area and takes off the line that was holding me. I freeze for a second, looking around. There are lots of things on the ground—playthings, I think. The other puppies start to play fighting and pulling on the toys. One little thing, half my size, grabs my tail and then tries to chew my foot! I won't let that happen. I grab the puppy's ear and give it a good chew. He yelps loudly. That will teach him!

I look around again. Every puppy seems to be having fun. They're all fighting over playthings, and some are even finding food inside the toys! Maybe this place isn't so bad after all. I decide to join in.

I jump into the fun, pulling on toys with the others, and even find some food inside one of the playthings. The best part? I meet some really nice puppies, and we start playing tug together. It's the best fun ever!

This place might not be so bad.

Explanation: Socialisation and Training

It's time for another explanation, so I'll step out of my puppy guise and back into my human state. The family has taken Rex to a puppy socialisation event at the vet's office, which explains the worrying smells. But this event helps Rex get used to the environment, so he begins to associate the building with more pleasure than pain.

The socialisation sessions are designed to help puppies get used to being around other dogs and people while also engaging their natural senses. For instance, the puppies learn to use their sense of smell to find food hidden inside toys. Over the next few weeks, Rex will be taught that play is fun, the vet isn't so scary, and other dogs can be great companions.

During these sessions, Rex will also start learning the body language of other dogs. While body language is instinctive, puppies still need to practice understanding the signals of play, curiosity, and even boundaries. As they interact, they will learn from each other, reinforcing these natural signs.

After each socialisation event, Rex will be exhausted—sleep will definitely be the order of the day! A quick trip outside to the toilet, and then he'll likely have a long, well-deserved rest. Soon, however, the next phase of his development will begin—formal training.

This training will help Rex become a "Good Citizen," as the UK Kennel Club calls it. This means he'll learn important skills like walking nicely on a lead, behaving around other dogs and people, and coming back when called. The key to this training is that Rex won't be forced to do anything—everything will be reward-based, using positive reinforcement. For instance, when Rex walks calmly beside Missy or Charlie, he'll be rewarded with a treat or a lot of praise. It's a method designed to be fun and engaging, ensuring Rex enjoys the process while building good habits.

Not only does this kind of training help Rex learn manners, but it also strengthens the bond between him and his family. Through positive reinforcement, Rex learns that good behaviour leads to rewards, making him eager to please and more connected with his humans.

Now that we've covered the training process, let's get back to the joys of puppyhood with Rex.

Feeling Worn Out

I'm flat out—so tired from these past few weeks. Ever since going to that smelly place, it's been non-stop! But it's been good. I've made so many new friends and learned lots of hooman sounds and barks. I hope we go back again and again.

But my mouth still hurts. It feels like my chewing bits are getting bigger, and more of them are popping up every day. Moomy gives me cold things to chew on, which helps, but the pain doesn't really go away. When I accidentally chew on the wrong things—like the humans—they squeak so loud, it hurts my ears! I try not to do it, but sometimes it just happens when I'm playing. It's automatic, really.

I've tried chewing on some of the hard things standing around the house, but that just makes the hoomans bark at me. Each time, they give me the long cold play thing instead. It does help with my aching mouth, but I still wish the pain would stop.

Rex's Final Day at Puppy Class

I've been waiting all day for this! I can tell when it's puppy class time—Missy and Shaarly get all excited and put on their extra skin coverings, and then the long-neck thing goes around me. That's when I knew we were going!

When we get there, I run straight inside. I can't wait to see all the other puppies! It smells just like it always does—like fun and food and a little bit of something else I can't quite name. Maybe that's just hooman smell? Who cares, I just want to play!

Today is as fun as always. We get to practise everything I've learnt—sitting when the big hooman makes that sound, coming back when Missy calls me (I get a bit distracted sometimes, but it's all part of the fun!). There are toys everywhere, and we chase each other, tug on ropes, and sneak bits of food from hiding places.

I'm getting really good at this. I know when the hooman wants me to sit or come, and I always get lots of praise. I love making them happy, especially when I get those yummy treats they call "shweetys."

But today feels a little different. There are more hugs from Missy and Shaarly, and the big hooman with a loud voice keeps talking to Moomy. I don't understand all their sounds, but I think they're planning something. Another game, maybe? Or more treats?

I'm not sure what's going on, but I'm having so much fun I don't even care. We finish up, and Missy gives me a long hug before we head back to the big noisy box.

I can't wait to come back again. Today was the best day yet!

Another Adventure

We're off again! I hope we're going to the play place. Sometimes we go out, and I think we're going, but the smells are all wrong. When that happens, Missy takes me with Shaarly. It's fun—Missy plays with me a lot, and I meet other small hoomans who want to cuddle and play.

I try to be nice, but sometimes they squeeze too tight, and I can't get away. I wriggle and wriggle, but I'm little, and they're big.

Playing with Shaarly is always good, though. He throws things for me to fetch, and I'm really fast at getting them! But when I bring it back, he keeps shouting at me. I got it, didn't I? So I'm keeping it!

Then I catch the smell — the smell. Yes! We're going to the play place! In we go, and all my puppy friends are here. I'm so excited!

Shaarly stands a little taller now, holding the long line that leads to my collar. His voice sounds excited, but he's trying to be serious as he says, "Rex, come!" That's the cue! The one that means I get to run!

I bolt forward, my paws pounding the ground as fast as they can. The wind whips past me, and I don't slow down — I'm charging toward Shaarly with all my might. I can see him bracing himself, but he's not ready for this. I'm coming in fast, and I can't stop myself!

I reach him in a second, my paws hitting his legs as I leap up to greet him. I bounce up and down, too excited to contain myself, almost knocking him over! Shaarly stumbles, trying to keep his balance, and I keep jumping, my tail wagging furiously. Why isn't he playing with me yet?

He looks a little embarrassed—his face turning red as he glances at the other hoomans—and then he barks, "Rex, sit!"

Sit. Oh! I know what that means! I've been practising this one. I stop bouncing and drop to the ground, my tail wagging under me as I sit perfectly in front of Shaarly.

For a moment, everything is quiet. Then I hear it—a loud clap, clap, clap from the hoomans around us.

They're slapping their paws together, making that noise they always make when they're happy.

Shaarly kneels down and pats my head. "Good boy, Rex!" he says, sounding proud, even though I almost knocked him over. His face is still red, but I know he's happy.

I look around at all the hoomans. Missy and the others are smiling, and everyone keeps clapping. I don't know why they're all so excited, but I'm happy I made them proud. I wag my tail even faster. I think I like this "sit" thing.

Walking to Heel: A New Challenge

After a few more weeks of training, things start to get more serious. I'm still allowed to run off sometimes, but now there's a new challenge: walking by my hoomans without pulling ahead. They call it "heel," and I hear it a lot when we're walking outside.

I'm excited to explore to smell everything around me, and sometimes, I forget what they want. When I try to run ahead, the line tightens, and I hear the sound: "Heel." It's always the same, calm but firm.

At first, I don't understand why I can't just go forward whenever I want. There are so many interesting smells up ahead! But whenever I pull, they make that same sound—"heel." And when I slow down, staying by their side, they say "good boy" in a slow, happy voice. I like hearing that. It feels good to make them happy.

One day, it's Daard walking me. He's holding the line this time, not Shaarly or Missy. I've gotten better at this "heel" thing, but I still get distracted sometimes. As we walk through the open park, I see a bird fly past, and my first instinct is to run after it. I lunge forward, my paws ready to chase, but then I hear it again—"heel."

I stop in my tracks and look up at Daard. His voice is calm, and he's looking down at me with a small smile.

He says "heel" again, and this time, I stay by his side, walking right next to him.

"Good boy," he says slowly, and I can hear how pleased he is. My tail wags and I feel proud. I'm getting the hang of this! Every time I stay close to him, I hear that calm "good boy," and it makes me want to keep doing it.

Training Continues

We keep practising, day after day. It's not just with Daard—sometimes it's Missy, Shaarly or Moomy. They all use the same sounds. "Heel" when I start to pull ahead, and "good boy" when I stay by their side. I'm learning to listen better every time.

On some days, they let me off the lead again, and I get to run as fast as I want. But even then, I know I'll hear "Rex, come!" when they want me to come back. And when I do, I always get that soft pat on the head and a slow "good boy" that makes my tail wag like crazy.

I like this new routine. It's fun to run, but I've started to enjoy walking next to my hoomans, too. They're always happy when I stay close, and that makes me happy too. I've learned that there's a balance—running free is great, but walking calmly with them feels good, too.

The training never really stops, but that's okay. I'm learning, bit by bit, and I know there are always more treats, more praise, and more "good boy" sounds waiting for me.

Chapter 5

A Trip to a Hooman Football Match

Today is different. There's excitement in the air, and everyone in the house is getting ready. I can feel the buzz in the air as Shaarly and Daard put on special skin coverings, ones I haven't seen before. Missy is excited, too, bouncing around the house, holding something with a strange smell—like leather but different. They keep calling it a *football*, and I keep hearing Shaarly bark something about a "match."

Before I know it, I'm clipped into my neck collar, and the long line is attached again. My tail starts wagging fast because I know this means we're going somewhere fun. We pile into the big noisy box, and this time, Missy sits next to me. I'm not sure where we're going, but the air smells different—like grass, mud, and something else... excitement.

When we get to the new place, everything is loud—really loud. The moment I hop out of the big box, I can hear hoomans barking from all directions. My ears twitch as I look around. There are so many people here, all shouting and clapping their paws together! It's almost too much for me to take in at once.

We walk toward a big open space where I see more hoomans standing on the side, watching something happening on a large patch of green stuff. Then I see it. In the middle of the field, there's a big, round ball—the ball! And there are hoomans running after it, kicking it around just like Shaarly does when we play.

My instincts kick in immediately. I want to run after that ball! It's so close, rolling and bouncing across the green stuff, just begging to be chased. My paws start moving on their own, and I pull forward, trying to run after it. But then—tug! The line pulls me back, and I hear the familiar sound from Daard.

"Rex, heel."

I stop and look up at him. He's holding the line tight, his hand on my neck collar, looking down at me with that calm, serious face. I know that sound. Heel means I can't run after the ball right now. I stay still, but I can't help the excitement bubbling up inside me. My tail wags, and I keep glancing at the ball. How can they expect me just to stand here when all those hoomans are chasing it?

Every time the ball moves, my legs tense. I want to go after it so badly. I hear Daard's calm voice again. "Heel, Rex," he says slowly, and I know I need to stay next to him.

It's hard—really hard. The hoomans are barking loudly all around me, and the big ball keeps rolling across the grass. But Daard is standing close, and every time I stay by his side, I hear the words I love: "Good boy."

The more I hear it, the more I realise it's okay. Even though I can't chase the ball, I'm doing something important by staying close to him. Still, I can't help but keep one eye on that ball. I feel the tug on the line each time I get a little too excited, and when I pull forward, I hear "heel" again.

There are moments when the noise gets louder, and all the hoomans around me start clapping and shouting at the same time. It's overwhelming, but I don't mind it too much. I watch as the ball moves up and down the field, and hoomans run after it, kicking and shouting. I can feel the excitement building in the air. Every now and then, Shaarly crouches down and pets my head, giving me a little more reassurance.

Suddenly, the ball comes flying toward the side where we're standing. It's so close now, rolling toward me with hoomans running right behind it! My legs spring into action before I even think, and I try to dart forward—this is my chance! But just as I move, Daard says it again— heel—and I stop, my paws skidding on the ground as I remember what I'm supposed to do.

I look up at him, and he's smiling. "Good boy, Rex," he says slowly, giving me a pat on the head. My tail wags furiously. The ball rolls past, but I don't chase it. I stay right where I'm supposed to be, and I feel a little proud. I wanted to chase that ball more than anything, but I knew Daard was happy with me for staying still.

The game goes on, and even though it's hard, I keep listening to the commands. Every time I hear "heel," I stay next to Daard, and every time I do, I get a slow "good boy" in return. The noise from the hoomans doesn't seem so bad anymore. I'm getting used to it, and I'm learning that sometimes, it's more important to listen than to chase after every ball I see.

A Special Day for Rex

There's something funny going on today. I can smell it in the air—delicious, warm smells drifting through the house, making my nose twitch with excitement. It's food, but not the kind I usually get in my bowl. This smells special like the food the hoomans sometimes have when other hoomans come over. I hear a lot of noises coming from the big room where the food is usually kept, and Missy and Shaarly are bouncing around with big smiles on their faces. They're excited, and I can feel the buzz of energy in the air.

The door opens, and that's when I smell something else—familiar scents! Visitors are arriving, and with them come the smells of other dogs... but not just any dogs. I know these smells! My tail wags as I sniff the air and recognise them—my friends from the fun class! The puppies I used to run and play with.

As the door opens wider, in they come, tails wagging and noses twitching, just like mine. I can hardly contain myself! I wiggle and squirm, wanting to greet each of them, sniffing their faces and tails. It's like the best surprise ever! All my puppy friends are here, and I can't believe my nose!

After a few moments of excitement inside, the hoomans start opening the big doors to the outside, and we all rush into the big green play area. The green stuff is soft beneath my paws, and I'm running before I even know where I'm going. My friends are all around me, chasing each other, tumbling in the grass, and pulling on toys. It's just like old times at the fun class, but better—because now, we're outside, and there's so much space to run!

I'm having the best time, darting between the other puppies, rolling in the grass, and tugging on ropes. It feels like we're running forever, and I don't want it to end. The sun is warm, the smells are exciting, and everything is perfect.

<u>Rex's Thoughts</u> - *Those birds think they're so cool just because they can fly. I'd like to see them try to fetch—that's real clever!*

But then, from a distance, I hear it—Missy's voice calling my name. "Rex! Come here, Rex!"

I stop in my tracks. I don't want to go in, not yet. I'm having too much fun! I glance around at my friends, still playing, and for a moment, I think about staying outside. But the sound of Missy's voice, full of excitement, makes me think. Maybe something good is happening inside? I give one last look at the other puppies before deciding to turn around and head toward the house.

As I get closer to the door, the smell of food hits me even stronger. My nose goes into overdrive, sniffing the air. It smells so good. When I step inside, something strange happens—all the hoomans start barking together. I can't understand what they're saying, but it sounds like, "Happy Birthday to you!"

Birthday? What does that mean?

I stop and look around, confused. Why are they all making the same noise? They're smiling and clapping their paws together, and as I step forward, they all start patting me on the head and back. Everyone seems so happy. Even Shaarly and Missy are beaming, their hands patting my sides as they keep saying that same sound—"Happy Birthday, Rex!"

I tilt my head, trying to understand. What did I do to make them so happy? Did I do something right? They're all giving me so much attention, patting me and smiling, and then, I see it—the treats!

Moomy is holding a plate of little treats, and she starts giving them to me and the other puppies. They're soft and delicious, and I gobble them up as fast as I can. My friends are eating their treats too, and it feels like a party—but I still don't know what the "Birthday" command means.

The hoomans keep barking the same sound—"Birthday"—and they're all so pleased. It's confusing, but it feels good. I must have done something right. Everyone is clapping, giving me treats, and patting my head. It's like the best day ever, and I'm starting to think this "Birthday" thing must be something important.

As I sit in the middle of all the excitement, surrounded by my friends, the smells of food, and all the hoomans smiling, I wag my tail. I don't understand everything, but I know one thing—they're happy. And when the hoomans are happy, I'm happy too.

Maybe I'll figure out what "Birthday" means one day, but for now, I'm just going to enjoy it. It sounds good, it smells good, and if it means more treats and fun like this, then I think I like this "Birthday" thing very much.

Back to being human again for a short explanation. It's the holiday season, and the Richardsons are preparing for a holiday week in Blackpool. It will be the first experience of sea and sand for Rex but he doesn't know it yet.

Day 1: Arriving in Blackpool

There's excitement in the air from the moment we arrive in Blackpool. The smell of salt fills my nose as soon as we step out of the car, and I can hear strange noises coming from somewhere nearby—like a deep rumbling mixed with splashing sounds. It's different from anything I've ever smelled or heard before. I wag my tail, eager to explore.

Missy and Shaarly are bouncing around with excitement, and Daard and Moomy look happy, too. We're heading toward the sound, and I can smell something else too—food! Everything smells different here. It's not like home.

As we walk, the ground beneath my paws starts to change. It's no longer hard like the pavement; it feels soft, and when I look down, I see that I'm standing on something strange. It's gritty and warm, and it shifts under my paws as I walk. I take a tentative step forward, my nose twitching, and realise it's all around me—sand! This stuff is so weird!

I run forward a little, feeling the sand move beneath me, and start digging at it with my paws. It's fun to push it around, and it feels nice and warm, but then I hear that strange rumbling noise again and stop to listen. Something is moving nearby, and I don't know what it is yet.

Day 2: First Encounter with the Sea

The next day, we head straight to the beach. The big, open space with all the sand is fun, but the thing that catches my eye is the huge, moving blue thing in front of us—the sea! It keeps coming towards me and then pulling away, making loud splashing sounds. I tilt my head, watching it. It moves so strangely, like it's alive!

I'm a little nervous. Every time the sea gets closer, I take a step back, not sure what to do. I can see it moving closer, then it pulls back. Missy and Shaarly are already running towards it, laughing and shouting. I can't understand why they're not afraid of it. The water comes right up to their feet, splashes them, and then pulls away.

Then, Shaarly steps into the water, and I stop and stare. He's walking right into the moving sea! I bark a little, trying to warn him, but he seems happy, splashing around. He looks back at me and waves me over, shouting, "Come on, Rex! It's fun!"

I'm not so sure. The water keeps moving, and I'm not sure if I like it. But Shaarly is in there, and he looks okay... I take a few slow steps forward, keeping my eyes on the water. It keeps moving, splashing up to my paws, and I jump back at first. It's cold and a little scary, but I look back at Shaarly, who's laughing and waving me forward.

So, I try again. This time, I step into the water and feel it cover my paws. It's cold and strange, but it's not as bad as I thought. I follow Shaarly in, a little nervous at first, but soon I'm splashing around with him, feeling the water move all around me. It's not too bad after all!

Day 3: Fun on the Beach

By the third day, I'm starting to enjoy the beach a lot more. We spend the whole day here, and I get to run around on the sand, dig holes, and chase after Shaarly and Missy. They throw a ball for me, and I race to get it, my paws kicking up sand behind me as I run.

The sea isn't as scary now either. I've been in a few times with Shaarly, and although I still think it's a bit strange how it moves, I like the cool feeling on my paws. We play by the shore, and I splash around, running in and out of the water. The hoomans seem happy, and every time I come back to them, they pet me and say, "Good boy, Rex!" That always makes me feel proud.

Day 4: A Taste of Ice Cream

Today, something really special happens. After a long morning of playing on the beach, we go to a little place near the water where there are lots of hoomans standing in line. I can smell something sweet and cold in the air, and it's making my nose twitch.

The hoomans call it ice cream, and I've never tasted anything like it. Missy kneels down and holds a little bit of it out to me, and I sniff it carefully before giving it a lick. The coldness surprises me at first—it's freezing! But then I taste the sweetness, and my tail starts wagging fast. I want more! I take another lick, and another, and soon I'm licking the whole thing up. It's delicious! I've never had anything so cold and sweet before.

The hoomans laugh as I lick my lips and wag my tail, and Missy gives me another small taste of the ice cream. It's the best treat I've ever had. I hope we get more of this ice cream stuff!

Day 5: Exploring the Pier

Today we go somewhere new—the pier. It's a long, wooden walkway that stretches out over the sea, and there are so many smells! There are food stands everywhere, and I can smell fried fish, chips, sweet things, and more of that delicious ice cream.

We walk along the pier, and I'm so excited by all the different smells that I can barely focus on where I'm going. Missy holds onto my lead to keep me close, but I can tell she's excited too. We stop at one of the stands, and I get a little taste of something fried—it's crunchy and salty, and I love it.

As we walk back, I can see the sea below us, moving just like before, but I'm not nervous this time. I know what it is now, and I'm not afraid.

Day 6: Rest and Relaxation

After so many days of running, splashing, and exploring, today is a little quieter. We still go to the beach, but I spend most of the day lying on a soft towel near Daard, watching the waves come in.

<u>Rex's Thought</u> - *It moves! It comes closer, then runs away. What is this water up to? Does it think I'm chasing it? Well, I'll play along—let's see if I can catch it this time!*

It's peaceful too, and I feel the warmth of the sun on my back as I drift in and out of sleep.

Every now and then, Missy or Shaarly come over to pet me or throw a ball, and I run after it, but mostly, I'm content just to relax. It's been a long week, and I'm starting to feel a little tired. But it's the good kind of tired, the kind that comes from having fun.

Day 7: One Last Splash

On our final day in Blackpool, we go back to the beach for one last playtime in the sand and sea. By now, I'm confident and happy to run in and out of the water, splashing around with Shaarly. The sea doesn't scare me anymore—in fact, I kind of like it!

We spend hours running, playing, and chasing balls, and when it's time to go, I don't want to leave. But I can tell the hoomans are happy, and that makes me happy too. As we pack up to leave, I take one last look at the sea, watching it move in and out like it always does.

It's been the best week ever, and I hope we come back to this sandy, splashy place again soon.

Rex's Thoughts - *Do hoomans think about squirrels as much as I do? Nah, probably not. They don't know what they're missing!*

The Day of the Kennel Club Bronze Test

Then came the big day. We arrived at the training school, and I could feel the excitement in the air. Shaarly was holding my lead tightly, and Missy was bouncing with excitement beside us. I could hear Daard telling Charlie to stay calm, but even I could sense how important today was.

We walked into the big room with other dogs and their hoomans. They all looked serious like something important was about to happen. I was just happy to be there. My nose twitched as I caught the familiar scents of my friends from training, but today, it felt different. Everyone was quieter and more focused.

Charlie bent down to my level, his face close to mine. "You ready, Rex?" he asked, giving me a pat on the head. I wagged my tail, happy to see him excited. He stood up straight and held my lead, and suddenly, it was time.

The instructor walked over and started giving instructions. Charlie and I began with the usual commands—walking beside each other, stopping when I heard "sit," and even staying still when Charlie walked away. Everything was familiar, but for some reason, it felt more important today. I just kept doing what I was told, and every time I did, I heard Charlie's voice saying, "Good boy, Rex!" That made my tail wag harder each time.

Then came the trickiest part—recall. Charlie walked away, leaving me with the instructor. I wanted to follow him so badly, but I remembered the "stay" command and waited, even though I was buzzing with energy. Then, from across the room, I heard Charlie's voice calling me, "Rex, come!"

That was my favourite part! I sprinted towards him as fast as I could, my paws barely touching the ground. When I reached him, he crouched down and hugged me tight, saying "good boy" over and over. I wagged my tail so hard I thought I might knock him over.

Chapter 6

Success and Confusion

After what felt like only a few minutes, it was over. The instructor smiled at Charlie and handed him a piece of paper. Charlie's eyes lit up, and Missy started clapping and jumping up and down, her eyes wide with joy. Then something strange happened—Missy's eyes filled with water, and she started crying, but she was smiling too.

"Charlie, we did it! We passed!" she shouted, hugging him tightly.

I wagged my tail, looking up at them both, confused. *What just happened?* Why were they so happy? I only did what they told me to do—sit, stay, come. That's what I always did. But now, everyone was clapping and smiling at me like I'd done something really special.

Charlie held the paper up proudly, grinning from ear to ear. It had a shiny bronze stamp on it and some words I didn't understand. "I can't believe we passed the Kennel Club Bronze Test!" Charlie exclaimed, holding the certificate like it was the most precious thing in the world.

"Rex did so well! I want to do the next one, Charlie! Can we go for the silver test?" Missy asked, wiping the happy tears from her eyes.

Charlie smiled at her but shrugged. "We'll see, maybe," he said, still looking down at the certificate with pride.

I looked from Charlie to Missy, still wagging my tail but not sure why. I hadn't done anything different from what I always did, but they were both so excited, and that made me happy, too. I stood by Charlie, feeling the warmth of his hand on my head as he patted me gently.

"Good boy, Rex," he said, his voice soft and proud.

I still didn't understand what had just happened, but if it made my family this happy, it must have been something good. I sat there beside Charlie, my tail still wagging, watching as Missy bounced around and Daard and Moomy smiled proudly. They all seemed so happy, and that made my heart swell with joy, even if I didn't know what the big fuss was about.

As we walked out of the training school, Charlie still holding onto his piece of paper, I felt proud too. I didn't understand what the "Bronze Test" meant, but I did know one thing—I was a good boy.

And that was all that mattered.

Home Sweet Home

Being at home now is the best feeling in the world. I have my own family, and even though they're not like me— they don't have fur, they walk on two legs, and they make funny sounds—I know they're my family. They take care of me, they love me, and I love them just as much.

There's always something happening around here. Some days are full of excitement with long walks, where I get to explore new smells and run in big open spaces.

Other days are quieter, with lots of cuddles from Missy and Shaarly, or lazy afternoons spent by Daard's feet while he reads one of those things with lots of paper.

I love all of it. The best part is how happy they seem when they're with me. When we go on walks together, I stay close to them, walking just like they taught me during training. I can feel how proud they are of me, especially when they smile and give me treats for being a "good boy." That's the best sound in the world—good boy. It makes my heart feel warm and my tail wags like crazy.

The training is something I've come to really enjoy. Every time we practice commands—whether it's sitting, staying, or coming when called—I know it makes my family happy, and that's what I love most of all. When Charlie or Missy tells me to "sit" or "heel," and I do it just right, their faces light up, and I get pats on the head and sometimes a yummy treat.

But it's not just about the rewards. It's about knowing that I'm making them happy. I can see it in their eyes, hear it in their voices, and feel it in the way they hold me close or pat me gently. I'd do anything to keep them happy, because they've given me a home, and they love me just the way I am.

We play a lot too. Missy loves to throw balls for me in the yard, and I chase them as fast as I can, bringing them back just to see her laugh and clap her hands. Shaarly likes to play tug with me, and even though I think I'm stronger, he always laughs when I pull on the rope toy as hard as I can.

Daard takes me on quiet walks in the mornings when the world is still waking up. The air is cool, and it feels like it's just the two of us. I stay close by his side, walking to heel like I've been taught, and sometimes he stops and gives me a pat, saying "good boy" in that calm voice of his. Those moments are peaceful, and I love knowing that he trusts me to stay by his side.

Even when we're not doing anything special, just being in the house with my family is enough. I have my spot where I like to sleep, and I can always count on someone coming by to give me a little scratch behind the ears or a soft word. I can feel the love in everything they do—when they feed me, play with me, or just sit with me in the quiet.

I may not understand all the things they say, but I understand how they feel. And I know that they love me, just as much as I love them. This is my home, my family, and I wouldn't want to be anywhere else.

A Strange Morning

This morning feels different—very different. When I wake up, everything is usually calm, quiet, and warm. But not today. Today, something is wrong.

I can hear Missy crying before I even open my eyes. That's the first thing I notice. She never cries like this, not unless something bad has happened. I lift my head from my bed and look around, confused. What's going on? I get up, my paws tapping lightly on the floor as I walk toward her, but before I can reach her, I hear Shaarly's voice. It's fast, urgent. He's rushing around, talking into a small thing in his hand—one of those things the hoomans always hold close to their ears. I've seen him use it before, but this time, the way he's talking into it makes me nervous. He doesn't sound happy.

My ears twitch. I can hear Daard too. He's downstairs, pacing, his voice low and worried. I don't understand what he's saying, but it's not the usual calm tone he uses. It's different. I want to find him, to make sure everything's okay, but I hear Missy's cries again and stop in my tracks.

I don't like this. Where's Moomy? Why isn't she here with us?

I move toward the stairs, hoping to see Moomy coming down, but she's still upstairs. Everything feels wrong, and I don't know what to do. I whine softly, trying to get someone's attention. I want to help, but I don't know how.

Then, all of a sudden, there's a loud, terrible noise. It's like a wailing sound, echoing through the house, and it makes my fur stand on end. The sound is so loud it hurts my ears, and I bark instinctively, wanting to make it stop. It's not like any noise I've heard before. I don't like it.

Shaarly rushes over to me and grabs my collar, pulling me gently toward the food room. "Come on, Rex," he says, his voice shaky, "you need to stay here for a bit." I don't want to go into the food room—I want to stay with them, to make sure they're all safe. But Shaarly is insistent, and before I know it, he's shut the door behind me.

I'm alone in the food room now, but I can still hear everything outside. Missy's crying hasn't stopped, and there are new sounds—strange voices, voices I don't recognise. They don't belong to my family. Who are these people? I bark loudly, letting them know I'm here. Whoever they are, they better not hurt my family.

My paws pace back and forth across the floor as I listen to the unfamiliar voices, mixed with Missy's cries and Daard's low, worried tones. What's happening? Why am I in here? Why can't I see them? My tail down and my heart pounding in my chest as I wait.

I bark again, louder this time, hoping they'll hear me and let me out. I don't know these voices, and I don't like the way they make me feel. The wailing noise is still going on, but it's farther away now, more distant. I don't understand what's happening, and I don't like being away from my family when something feels so wrong.

Finally, after what feels like forever, the door opens. Shaarly comes in, and I rush over to him, nuzzling my head into his side, needing to know everything is okay. He kneels down, stroking my back softly. His voice is quieter now, calmer, but he still looks upset.

"It's okay, Rex," he says, patting my head. "Everything's going to be okay." His hand trembles a little as he pets me, and I can see in his eyes that something isn't right. But I don't understand what. What's "okay"? What happened? Where is Moomy? Why was Missy crying?

I sit beside Shaarly, my head resting on his leg as he continues to stroke my fur. I don't know what's going on, but I can feel how worried he is. I look up at him, confused, wanting to make him feel better, but I don't know how.

He stands up after a moment, walking over to the door. I follow him out, my tail wagging softly, trying to stay close. The house feels quieter now, but there's still something heavy in the air, something I can't quite place. I keep looking around, searching for Moomy, hoping she'll come down the stairs any minute.

But she doesn't.

Context: A Difficult Time for the Family

This is a difficult time for Rex and the family. Mrs. Richardson has been taken to the hospital and will need to stay there for a while. She has been diagnosed with cancer and requires treatment. The house feels different now, and the usual routines have been disrupted. Rex, with his sensitive nature, can feel the change even though he doesn't understand it. He knows something is wrong, but he doesn't know what, and he's upset that he can't find Mrs. Richardson—his Moomy. The days pass, and Rex grows more confused and worried as he searches for her, unsure of where she has gone or why the family seems so upset.

Rex's Confusion and Concern

The house feels strange these days. It's quieter, and everyone seems a little... different. Missy isn't bouncing around like she usually does, and Shaarly seems distracted all the time. Even Daard doesn't seem quite like himself. I've noticed it, but what worries me most is that I haven't seen Moomy for a while now. She's always here in the mornings, giving me my food and patting my head, but now... she's gone.

I don't understand where she is, and every day, I search the house for her. I look in all the usual places—upstairs, in the soft room where she likes to sit, in the big room where the food smells come from—but she's nowhere to be found. I even sit by the door sometimes, waiting, hoping she'll come back, but the door stays closed, and I'm left feeling confused and worried.

The family seems sad. I can hear it in the way they talk to each other, softer than usual. Missy cries sometimes, and when I go to her, she holds me tight, burying her face in my fur. I try to make her feel better, licking her face gently, but I don't know why she's crying. Where is Moomy? Why isn't she here to fix everything?

Shaarly tries to keep things normal. He still takes me on walks, but even then, it's not the same. He doesn't play with me as much, and sometimes, he talks to me in that soft, sad voice. I stay close to him on our walks, hoping he'll tell me what's going on, but the words he uses are still just sounds to me. I don't know what they mean, but I can feel the sadness in them.

When we get home, I go back to looking for Moomy. I check the places I've already searched, hoping maybe she'll be there this time, but she isn't. I sniff the air, catching her scent in the places she used to be, but it's fading, and that makes me even more anxious. I miss her, and I don't know why she isn't here with us.

Sometimes, I hear the family talking about a place called the "hospital." I don't know what that is, but I think it's where Moomy is. I can tell by the way they say it and the way their voices drop when they talk about it. It's not a happy place, wherever it is, and I don't like it.

Daard has been quiet, too. He spends a lot of time sitting alone, looking worried, and I try to sit next to him, leaning my head on his leg to let him know I'm here. He pats me absently, but his mind seems far away. I wish I could help. I wish I could make things better, but I don't know how.

Chapter 7

Days Passing Without Moomy

The days feel long without Moomy here. The routines are still the same, but they're different now. Missy and Shaarly try their best, but I can feel the change. Every day I wait, hoping she'll come home, but every day it's the same. I don't understand why she's not here or why everyone seems so sad.

I've started sleeping by the door at night, just in case she comes back. Sometimes I dream of her, of her soft voice calling my name, of her hand patting my head. But when I wake up, it's still quiet, and she's still not here. I don't know how long this will last. I don't know when Moomy will come back, but I'll keep waiting. I'll keep searching because I know she won't leave us forever. And in the meantime, I'll stay close to my family. They need me now more than ever, even if I don't understand why.

A Visit to the Hospital

Today feels different. There's a new kind of energy in the air, and I can sense the excitement mixed with a bit of worry. Daard, Shaarly, and Missy are getting ready, and I'm going with them. I don't know where we're going, but the way they're moving around, it feels important. We all pile into the big, noisy box, and I settle down on the seat next to Shaarly. I'm happy to be with them, and the thought crosses my mind—maybe we're going to see Moomy! That thought makes my tail thump against the seat in excitement. I've been waiting so long to see her again, to hear her voice and feel her hand pat my head like she always does.

The drive is quiet, but I can tell everyone is thinking about something important. I look up at Shaarly, but his face is focused, staring out the window as we drive. Missy, sitting in the back with me, is unusually quiet too. I lean against her, offering the only comfort I know how to give. When we finally stop, I smell something strange—lots of people, lots of different scents, and something else... something sterile and unfamiliar. My nose twitches as I try to figure out where we are. We step out of the car, and the air is filled with new sounds—machines beeping, voices talking quickly, doors opening and closing. We walk toward a large building, and the closer we get, the more certain I am that Moomy must be inside. My tail starts wagging faster. I haven't seen her in so long, and I miss her. But as we reach the entrance, something unexpected happens.

Daard stops, talking to a person at the door. I don't understand the words they're saying, but after a few moments, I can tell something is wrong. The person is pointing at me, and Daard's voice changes—it's more serious now. I look up, confused, not sure what's going on. Why can't I go in? Moomy is in there, I know it! Then, Shaarly speaks up, his voice sharp with frustration. "What do you mean he can't come in? He's family!" I hear the person respond, but I don't understand the words. They sound calm, but they're still pointing at me.

My tail droops a little, and I look at Shaarly, trying to understand. Why can't I go inside with them? The person explains something to Shaarly, but I only catch a few words that make sense to me. Shaarly turns to Daard and repeats what the person says. "They said Rex can't come in because he's not a Therapy Dog."

Therapy Dog? I tilt my head. What's that?

Shaarly, looking frustrated, asks, "What do you mean, 'Therapy Dog'? He's trained—he's a good dog!"

The person at the door smiles softly, explaining, "A Therapy Dog is a special type of dog. They're trained to visit hospitals like this one to comfort sick adults and children. Only Therapy Dogs are allowed inside. They're trained to stay calm in medical environments and give comfort to patients. Rex is a wonderful dog, but he's not trained for this kind of work."

I hear the words, but I don't understand all of them. I only know that something is wrong. Why can't I go in with my family? I want to see Moomy to make sure she's okay.

Shaarly sighs, rubbing his hand through his hair. He crouches down beside me and pats my head. "It's okay, Rex. We'll go see Moomy, but you'll have to wait in the car, okay?"

I don't want to go back to the car. I want to stay with them. I want to see Moomy. My tail droops even more as Shaarly takes my lead and gently leads me away from the entrance. I look back at the door, watching as Daard and Missy disappear inside. I whine softly, not understanding why I can't follow them.

Shaarly opens the car door, and I hop back in, still confused. He strokes my head softly, his eyes sad. "I know, boy. I know you miss her." He stays with me for a few moments, patting me gently, but then he closes the door and heads back toward the hospital.

As I watch him walk away, I curl up on the seat, feeling a little lost. I don't know what a "Therapy Dog" is, but I wish I could be one. I wish I could go inside and see Moomy. Maybe I could make her feel better. After all, that's what I always try to do for my family.

Shaarly's Curiosity About Therapy Dogs

Later that night, after they've all come home from the hospital, Shaarly is still thinking about what the person said. He sits at the table, his fingers tapping on his small hand-thing, searching for something. I watch him, sensing his curiosity. He seems quieter than usual, deep in thought.

Finally, he speaks to Daard. "Dad, what if we trained Rex to be a Therapy Dog? Do you think he could visit Mummy then?"

Daard looks up, surprised but thoughtful. "Therapy Dog training is very specific, Shaarly. It takes a lot of time and patience. Rex is a great dog, but it's a big commitment. We need to complete his Kennel Club certificates first."

Shaarly's face is serious. "I know. But Rex is already such a comfort to us. I think he'd be amazing at it."

Daard nods slowly. "It's something to think about. Let's talk more about it. For now, Rex can stay by our side and help us here at home."

Moomy's Return

Another day without Moomy. It's getting harder to understand why she's not here. I've been worried for so long, and every time I search for her, she's never there. I miss her. I miss the way she pats my head, the way her voice sounds when she says, "Good boy." I miss everything about her, and I don't know where she's been.

But today feels different.

Missy is up really early, and there's something strange about her energy. She's smiling, but she looks anxious too. I wag my tail, picking up on her excitement, but I don't understand why she's up so early. Soon, I see Daard coming downstairs, putting on his outside cover. Shaarly is doing the same. Everyone is moving quickly, and I can't figure out what's going on.

Are we going for a walk? I think, hopefully, my tail is wagging faster. But something is different this morning. It's not the same routine. Normally, we would go for a walk first, but today is different. I watch as Shaarly grabs my lead, and we all head for the big moving box. My tail wags, though I'm still not sure what's happening. It feels odd, but I'm excited to be going with them.

We drive for a while, and soon, I realise we're back at the place they wouldn't let me go last time. My ears twitch with recognition, and my tail slows as I stare out the window. What are we doing here again? I remember the last time we came, how Daard and Missy went inside without me. I don't like this place. It feels... strange. And Moomy isn't here. At least, I haven't seen her yet.

Daard gets out of the big box and walks toward the building. He leaves us in the car, and I watch him through the window, still confused. My heart beats faster as I look around, wondering what's happening. Shaarly and Missy are sitting quietly, but I can tell something big is going on.

And then, after a little while, I see her.

Moomy!

She's coming toward us, and my heart nearly leaps out of my chest. I can barely contain myself. There she is! My Moomy! She's not walking as fast as usual, and she doesn't look as bright as I remember, but she's here. She's really here!

I start jumping around in the car, my paws scratching against the seat as I try to get closer to the door. Missy and Shaarly are both excited too, but Missy starts crying again, tears streaming down her face as she opens the door and jumps out of the car. Shaarly is holding onto my lead, trying to keep me calm, but I can't stop wagging my tail, barking, and pulling to get closer to her.

Shaarly is being very grown-up now, just like Daard. He holds on to me tightly, even though I'm pulling as hard as I can, desperate to reach Moomy. She's moving slowly, but she's coming toward us, and I can hardly believe it. I've missed her so much, and now she's here, and I can't hold back my joy.

When Moomy finally reaches us, I jump up and down, my tail wagging so hard it feels like it might fall off. I can't stop myself—I'm all over the place, licking Missy, jumping on Shaarly, barking, and turning in circles. I don't even know what to do with all the excitement bubbling inside me.

Moomy smiles at me, and I can see that she's tired, but her hand reaches out to pat my head, and at that moment, everything feels right again. She's back. She's here with us, and I can't stop the happiness from overflowing. I bark and wag my tail, trying to show her how much I've missed her. She doesn't even need to say anything. Just seeing her is enough.

Missy is still crying, but she's smiling too, and I can tell these are happy tears. Shaarly holds me steady, stroking my back as we all stand there together, reunited. I look up at him, and he smiles down at me, his voice soft. "It's okay, Rex. She's home."

Home. That's all I need to hear. Moomy is coming home, and everything feels right again.

<u>Rex's Thoughts</u> - *I wagged my tail so much, I think I made the air happier!*

Chapter 8

Out of Dog Mode: Life Moves Forward

In the months that follow, life continues with both challenges and small victories for Rex and the Richardson family. Mrs. Richardson has to visit the hospital regularly for ongoing treatment. The days are difficult, especially for the family, as they adjust to a new routine centred around hospital trips, doctor visits, and Mrs. Richardson's recovery. Despite the struggles, they find ways to support each other and keep life as normal as possible.

During this time, Rex's training progresses significantly. He continues his Kennel Club training with dedication, easily passing his Silver and Gold tests. These certificates now hang proudly on the wall, a testament to Rex's growth, hard work, and the strong bond he shares with his family. However, his progress in training also brings a bittersweet moment—his last class with his doggie friends. Saying goodbye to the other dogs was a sad day for Rex; he had looked forward to those weekly meetups and enjoyed the play and camaraderie with his friends. Still, Rex remains loyal to his family, understanding that his most important role is at home, especially now.

As Mrs. Richardson continues her treatment, Rex intuitively senses that she needs him more than ever. He's always been a source of comfort for the family, but now he has adopted a new habit that reflects his deep loyalty and love. Every night, he settles down on the floor next to Mooms bed. It's his chosen spot—right by her side, where he can stay close. He knows she's feeling weak and tired, and he wants to be there for her. Sometimes, when she reaches out for comfort, her hand finds him resting on his soft fur. Rex doesn't need to understand the full extent of her illness—he knows his presence helps, that just being there for her is enough to make her feel less alone during the difficult days.

Even though life has changed, Rex has grown into a calm, dependable part of the family, offering quiet support. His presence in the house provides a sense of stability for everyone.

While Mrs. Richardson's journey to recovery continues, Rex's gentle companionship is a constant reminder of love, loyalty, and the quiet power of being there for someone in their time of need.

A New Adventure Begins

One day, the routine changes again. I've been feeling things slowly returning to normal around the house. Moomy is still tired some days, but she smiles more, and the family seems calmer. And today, something special happens. Missy grabs my lead and clips it onto my collar. I wag my tail, excited for another adventure. But this isn't just any walk. I can feel the difference in the air.

Missy, Daard, and I head out to the big moving box, and I jump in, eager to go wherever they're taking me. As we drive, I start to recognise the scent. The further we go, the more familiar it feels. The training school! My tail thumps against the seat in excitement. Are we going back? Will I see my friends again? I loved those classes—running, playing, learning new things.

But when we arrived, something was different.

I look around, my tail slowing as I take it all in. The familiar place is still there—the big open space, the room where I learned to sit and stay—but where are my friends? I don't see them. It's just me, Daard, Missy, and the teacher. The teacher is standing there, smiling at me, but I'm confused. Where are the other dogs?

Daard and Missy walk up to the teacher, and I sit down, trying to figure out what's going on. I can hear the adults talking, but I don't understand all of it. Their barks go back and forth, and I look up at Daard, hoping for some clue as to what's happening.

Then, I hear it again—that funny word I've heard before. "Therapy."

My ears perk up at the sound. I've heard them say it before, but I still don't know what it means. I tilt my head, trying to make sense of it. The teacher is looking at me, then at Missy, then back to Daard. They're talking, and I catch little bits of it. I hear the word "training" again, and Daard points at me and then at Missy.

Missy is standing beside me, looking anxious. She's holding onto my lead a little tighter than usual, and I can feel her nervous energy through the line. I look up at her, wagging my tail softly, trying to reassure her. I don't know what's going on, but I trust her. Whatever this is, I'll be there for her, just like I've always been.

The teacher bends down to my level, giving me a pat on the head. Her voice is calm and soft like she's explaining something important. I don't understand all the sounds, but I can tell by the way she's looking at me and the way Daard and Missy are watching that this is something new.

I sniff the air, still trying to piece together what's happening. The word "Therapy" keeps coming up, and the way they say it makes me think it's something good—something I'm supposed to help with. I don't fully understand, but I know one thing: I'll do anything to make my family happy. If this is something they want me to learn, then I'm ready.

The teacher stands up and starts gently talking to Daard again. Missy looks down at me and smiles a little, her anxiety starting to fade. She kneels beside me, stroking my fur. "You'll be great, Rex," she whispers, her voice soft but full of warmth.

I don't know exactly what's happening, but the calm energy in the room starts to settle into me too. Maybe this is a new kind of training? Something like the Kennel Club tests, but different. Something called Therapy. And even though I don't understand the details, I know one thing for sure—I'm ready for whatever comes next.

Therapy Dog Training: Why Rex is Here

The decision to bring Rex into Therapy Dog training was one that Mr. Richardson made after seeing how much comfort Rex had brought to the family during Mrs. Richardson's illness. Rex had been a constant source of emotional support—

not just for Mrs. Richardson but for the entire family. His calm, loving presence during the most difficult times made it clear that Rex had a unique gift.

After noticing how naturally Rex provided comfort, Daard contacted an organization called Pets As Therapy to learn more about the possibility of Rex becoming a certified Therapy Dog. Pets As Therapy is a charity that trains dogs to provide emotional support to people in hospitals, care homes, schools, and other settings where people might need companionship and comfort. Therapy Dogs like Rex are trained to help both children and adults, offering emotional relief and improving well-being simply by being there.

The decision to enroll Rex in the Therapy Dog program came from a place of wanting to share the comfort and love he provided at home with others who might benefit from his calming presence. After speaking with the Pets As Therapy team, Daard learned that Rex would need to undergo specialised training and pass a series of tests to ensure he was ready for the demands of being a Therapy Dog.

What Therapy Dog Training Involves

Therapy Dog training focuses on developing key behaviours that allow dogs to remain calm and composed in a variety of settings, no matter how unpredictable or stressful they might be. The goal is for Rex to maintain his calm demeanour, even when surrounded by strange environments, loud noises, and unusual smells. Here's what Rex would need to master during his training:

1. **Remaining Calm in Unfamiliar Situations**: *Rex will be introduced to a range of unfamiliar environments. This includes hospitals, care homes, schools, and other places that may have strange, sometimes unpleasant smells. Rex will need to remain composed and confident in these new settings, ensuring that he can bring calm to those around him instead of becoming anxious.*

2. **Responding Calmly to Loud Noises**: *Loud noises are a common occurrence in places like hospitals or schools. Rex must learn to stay calm if something*

sudden, like a tray of cups falling or a door slamming, happens near him. Instead of becoming startled or agitated, Rex needs to look calmly at the situation and stay in place, showing people that they can rely on his stable presence.

3. **Gentle Interaction with Children**: Many Therapy Dogs visit schools or paediatric wards, where they interact with children. Rex will need to demonstrate that he can handle cuddles from children without becoming agitated. Children might not always know how to handle dogs gently—they might pull on their ears or fur, but Rex's training will teach him to walk away calmly instead of reacting. This is important because children in therapy situations can sometimes act unpredictably, and a Therapy Dog must respond with patience.

4. **Managing Loud, Busy Environments**: Hospitals, care homes, and schools can be noisy, chaotic places. Rex's training will teach him how to stay focused

and calm, even when there are loud voices, running children, or medical equipment making strange noises around him. He must learn to stay composed, providing a sense of comfort to those who need it most.

5. ***Appropriate Behaviour Around Children****: While Rex may be used to playing with Shaarly and Missy, his therapy work will involve a different kind of interaction with children. In schools or therapy settings, Rex must learn to wait calmly for children to come to him. Some children may be nervous or scared of dogs, so Rex will need to remain calm, sitting quietly until the child is ready to approach him. His calm energy can help ease a child's fear or anxiety, giving them the confidence to interact with him on their own terms.*

6. ***Visiting Hospitals and Care Homes****: As a Therapy Dog, Rex will likely visit hospitals and care homes where people are feeling unwell or lonely. His training will prepare him for these emotionally charged environments. He will learn how to approach patients*

gently, allowing them to pet him, hold his paw, or simply feel his presence nearby. In care homes, he may be spending time with elderly residents who benefit from his quiet companionship.

The Importance of a Therapy Dog's Role

Therapy Dogs like Rex are trained to bring emotional relief to people who are experiencing difficult times—whether they are sick, recovering, or simply in need of companionship. By remaining calm and offering non-judgmental support, Therapy Dogs can improve people's mental health and well-being. Rex, with his naturally comforting demeanour, is a perfect candidate for this kind of work, and the training will help him develop the skills he needs to help others in a meaningful way.

Daard and Missy know that this training is an important step for Rex. They've seen firsthand how much comfort he brings to Mrs. Richardson during her recovery, and they believe that Rex can bring that same sense of peace to others who need it. As Rex continues his training, they are hopeful that one day he will become an official Therapy Dog, visiting hospitals, care homes, and schools to provide the same love and comfort to others that he has given to his family.

Back to Being Rex: Therapy Dog Training

I've been going to this new kind of training for what feels like a lot of times now. It's different from the classes I used to go to with all the other dogs. This time, it's just me—no friends to run around with or tug toys. I miss the other dogs sometimes, but I know this is important because Missy and Mr. Richardson are always there, and I can tell they're watching me closely.

At first, I found it really hard not to want to play, especially when children were around. They're always moving so fast, laughing and giggling, and I just want to run with them, wagging my tail and jumping around. But Missy's voice cuts through the excitement. "No, sit." She's getting really good at this training stuff, almost as good as Shaarly. I hear her command, and even though my legs twitch, wanting to run, I sit down like she asked. I can feel her calm energy through the lead, and I try my best to match it.

It's strange being in this new type of training—no dogs, just lots of people—sometimes adults, sometimes children. I miss the running and playing, but there's something special about this too. I've noticed that when I stay calm and do what Missy or Mr. Richardson asks, the people around me seem happy. They come over, give me soft strokes on my back, and sometimes even hug me. I like that part a lot.

I'm trying hard to remember all the things they've been teaching me. One of the hardest things is staying calm when there's a lot of noise. The other day, during training, there was a really loud crash. I jumped—who wouldn't?—but Missy was quick. She said, "Still," and even though my heart was racing, I stayed right next to her. I wanted to bark or run, but I trusted her. I looked up at her, and she looked so calm, so I just sat there, waiting.

After a while, I realised nothing bad was happening. It was just the teacher dropping something.

Missy gave me a pat and whispered, "Good boy," and I felt so proud. It's hard sometimes, not reacting to loud noises or strange smells, but every time I do it right, I can feel how happy Missy and Mr. Richardson are. That makes it worth it.

I also really enjoy the people who come to visit during the training sessions. They come over, smile at me, and give me hugs and strokes. Some of them seem sad at first, but when they pet me, I can feel them relax, like I'm making them feel better. That's new for me—usually, it's my family who makes me feel better. Now, it feels like I'm the one helping. I don't always understand everything, but I can sense that just sitting there, being still and calm, makes a big difference to them.

But it's also a little confusing. No other dogs come in to play or train with me. At first, I wondered why I was the only one, but now I'm starting to realise this training isn't about playing with other dogs—it's about being there for the hoomans. It's about making them feel safe and happy.

Missy's getting better at giving me commands. She's confident now when she says "Sit" or "Stay," and I can tell she's proud of me when I listen right away. Sometimes, I look at her, and she's got that same proud look Shaarly used to have when he first taught me how to fetch or heel.

So, even though it's different from what I'm used to, I'm starting to enjoy this new kind of training. I still miss running and playing with other dogs, but I'm learning that this is important. I'm learning how to stay calm, even when there's noise or movement or new people around. And every time someone smiles at me or gives me a soft pat after I've been good, I know I'm doing something right.

This might not be the kind of fun I'm used to, but it's something else—a kind of joy that comes from knowing I'm helping. And as long as Missy, Mr. Richardson, and all these new hoomans are happy, that's what matters most to me.

Chapter 9

A Surprise with Moomy

We just got back from another training session, and I'm feeling pretty proud of myself. Missy keeps telling me I'm doing such a good job, and I love hearing those words. But today feels special, different. As soon as we get home, Daardy says we're all going out—*with Moomy*! I don't know where we're going, but I'm already wagging my tail because I know if Moomy is coming, it's going to be fun.

Moomy's been tired a lot lately, and I haven't seen her this excited in a while. She's smiling more today, and even though she's moving a bit slower than usual, she looks happy. We all pile into the big moving box—me, Missy, Shaarly, Daardy, and, of course, Moomy—and off we go. I can feel the excitement buzzing in the air. I don't know where we're going, but I know it's going to be good.

When we stop, I jump out, sniffing the air. This place looks kind of like where we live—lots of green grass, trees, and space to run—but something is different. There's a familiar scent in the air, one that makes my tail wag even harder.

Could it be?

We walk inside, and that's when I see them—*my doggie friends*! They're all here! I can hardly believe it! It's been so long since I've seen them, and I'm practically bouncing with excitement. I tug a little on my head, wanting to run over, but I stop when I see something even more important happening.

All the hoomans—my family, my doggie friends' hoomans—are gathered around Moomy. They're all barking happily, making excited sounds, and hugging her. Some of my doggie friends are licking her hands and wagging their tails so fast it's like they might take off into the air. I can hear the happy barks of all the hoomans around, and Moomy is laughing, her face full of joy.

Missy is crying again. She's always crying, but this time, I think it's the good kind of crying. She's holding onto Moomy tightly like she doesn't want to let go. Moomy hugs her back, and I can see it—*she's better*. She looks as happy as she ever was, and her smile is bigger than I've seen in a long time.

I look up at Missy, and even though her eyes are wet, she's smiling too. The kind of smile that makes me want to wag my tail even more.

It's hard to stay still with all this excitement going on. My hooman friends are all so happy, and I can feel it buzzing through me. Moomy really does seem better, and that makes me feel so happy inside like my heart is wagging as much as my tail. I just can't contain myself anymore.

I glance up at Missy, and she nods, finally letting go of my lead. That's all I need—I take off like a rocket, zooming out to the big green area where my doggie friends are running. I bark happily as I race around, feeling the wind in my fur. The grass is soft beneath my paws, and the sun is shining just right.

We all chase each other, tugging on toys and rolling around in the grass. It's just like the old times, before all the hospital visits and the quiet days. I can hear the laughter of the hoomans in the background, their voices mixing with the happy barks of my friends.

Everything feels right again. Moomy is happy, Missy and Shaarly are smiling, and I'm surrounded by my best friends, running in the sunshine.

What a great time.

The Morning Walk

The next day starts early, as usual. Daardy is up, and that means it's time for my favourite morning routine: the early walk. There's something special about these early morning walks, and it's not just about stretching my legs.

<u>Rex's Thought</u> – *The smells out here are like a storybook for my nose. I can tell which dogs passed this way, what they had for breakfast, and even which squirrel forgot where they buried their nut!*

Out of Doggie mode for an explanation.

First thing in the morning, everything feels fresh. The world is waking up, but before it does, so much has already happened during the night. It's like a whole other world unfolded while everyone was sleeping. Urban foxes have passed through, cats have wandered around, and people have left traces of their footsteps, moving in and out of their homes. And the best part for dogs? They get to smell it all.

I like to think of it as a dog's version of the morning newspaper. While we might check our phones or grab a cup of coffee to catch up on the latest news, dogs check in on their surroundings by using their noses. Every scent tells a story—whether it's a fox that wandered through, a neighbour's dog that passed by, or a cat that snuck through a garden.

For dogs, it's a way of keeping up with the world around them. It's how they figure out what's happened overnight, which dogs have been in the area, and what new developments there might be in the neighbourhood. It's their version of a "newspaper run," and just like we do, they like to "read" what's going on first thing in the morning.

Back to the walk

Daardy and I head out into the quiet morning, and I'm immediately drawn to the scents all around me. The cool air is filled with stories from the night—paw prints left behind by cats, foxes marking their territory, and the familiar scent of other dogs who have already walked this path. Each sniff is a new discovery, a way of catching up with what's been happening while we are all asleep.

For hoomans, this might seem like a simple walk, but for dogs, it's a morning ritual full of information. It's how we stay connected to our world, and it's one of the reasons these early walks are so important.

A New Adventure with Missy and Moomy

A few sleeps have passed, and things feel a bit different lately. I've noticed that Shaarly isn't around as much. He seems to go out on his own a lot these days, and I miss him sometimes. But Missy is still here, and she's been keen on training me some more. She's always watching me closely, giving me commands, and I can tell she's proud when I get things right. Today, she seems especially excited about something. I can see it in the way she's moving, all quick and eager, and that gets my tail wagging too.

Oh wait—she's getting my line! That's always a good sign. And Moomy is putting her cover on too. *Yippee! We're going out again!*

I can barely contain my excitement as we head to the big moving box. Today feels extra special because Moomy is sitting in Daard's seat. I've never seen her there before! I don't know where we're going, but with Missy and Moomy, it's bound to be fun.

The drive takes a little while, and I start thinking about where we might be headed. Maybe we're going to the big green place where children play, or maybe it's another day of training. Could it be a visit to see my doggie friends? I don't know, but I can't stop my tail from wagging in anticipation.

We stop at a building I've never been to before. It's smaller than the places we usually visit—not like a home for hoomans, but more like the training place. Missy gets me out of the box with Moomy by her side, and we head inside. The smells here are new, and I'm curious but also a bit unsure.

Inside, there's a big hooman I've never met before. He's kind of like Daard—big but with a gentle face. He kneels down to greet me, which makes me feel a bit more comfortable, though for a second, I wonder—Are they giving me away?

But then I hear him say that word again—therapy. I've heard it a few times now, and every time they say it, something important happens. The big hooman barks gently to Missy, and I can see her listening carefully. We go through some of my routines, like we always do in training—sit, stay, calm—but then, suddenly, there's a big crash behind me! I jump a little, my heart racing, but I hear Missy's voice say, "Calm, sit," and I remember my training. I sit down and try my best to stay calm, just like I've been taught. When I finally look behind me, I see it's just a big bowl—kind of like the one I feed from—only this one has a lot of shiny things in it.

The big hooman barks gently to Missy again, and she puts her cover back on. We leave the building and head home, but I'm still not quite sure what just happened. It felt like training again, but a little different. Either way, Missy seemed happy, so I must've done well.

A Special Morning and Something New

A few more sleeps go by, and then, one morning, something unusual happens. Missy wakes up early and goes to the opening that leads outside. She moves the big swing that blocks the opening and suddenly comes running back inside, calling everyone and shouting very loudly.

"Rex Barshed! Rex Barshed!" she yells, her voice full of excitement. That's me! I don't understand why she's calling my name so loudly, but it seems important.

Before I know it, Missy is putting something bright and shiny on my back—a jacket of some kind. I look down at it, thinking, *I don't really need a skin cover like hoomans do,* but Missy seems excited about it, so I let her put it on. Then she changes my neckwear too, and it feels... different. I'm not sure what's happening, but everyone is clapping and smiling, and I'm getting lots of pats and strokes.

It feels good—really good. I wag my tail harder, happy that I did something right, even though I'm not entirely sure what I did! The whole family is cheering for me, and I can see how proud they are, especially Missy. That makes me feel proud too.

I may not fully understand what just happened, but one thing's for sure—everyone is happy, and that's all that matters to me. Whatever this new bright jacket and new neckwear mean, I'll keep doing my best to make my family proud.

Rex's New Role: A Fully Fledged Therapy Dog

Let's step out of Rex's perspective for a moment to explain the importance of this day. After months of dedicated training, Rex has finally completed his journey to becoming a fully certified Pets As Therapy dog. The bright yellow jacket—or tabard—he now wears proudly has 'Pets As Therapy' written across the back, making it clear that Rex is no ordinary dog. His new collar, also bright yellow, features an ID tag with his picture on it, identifying him as a trained, tested, and fully qualified Therapy Dog.

This marks a huge moment for Rex and his family. The big celebration you've just read about reflects the pride and joy they feel, knowing Rex has officially become something truly special. Not only has Rex been a source of immense comfort and support to his own family, especially to Mrs. Richardson during her illness, but now, with his certification, he can extend that same comfort to others.

Mrs. Richardson, in particular, is more than pleased with this outcome. Having spent a lot of time in the hospital for her treatment, she saw firsthand how lonely and difficult it could be for the other patients, especially children. Rex was such a comfort to her during those hard days, and now he can bring that same sense of peace and joy to the people and children who need it most—just as he did for her.

For Rex, the jacket and collar represent more than just training—they represent his new purpose. Wherever he goes now, whether it's a hospital, a care home, or a school, Rex will bring comfort, warmth, and companionship to those who need it most. The family's celebration is not just for Rex's success but for the fact that he's now part of something bigger, helping people beyond his own home.

Rex's First Therapy Visit

I've had my bright yellow back cover for a while now, and today feels different. Missy is putting it on me, along with my new neckband, but she seems a little nervous. Her hands are a bit shaky as she clips the line to my collar, and I look up at her, trying to reassure her with a wag of my tail. Moomy is putting on her cover too, and I can sense the excitement and nervousness in the air. Something important is happening today. I don't fully understand it, but I know we're going somewhere, and everyone is focused.

Daard is coming along as well, which means this is definitely something special. We all pile into the big box, and I settle down on the seat, trying to figure out where we're going. It's a bit of a journey, so I lay down and rest for a while, though every now and then, the box turns, and I nearly fall off the seat!

Eventually, we stop after a few turns, and when I stand up and sniff the air, I realise something—I've been here before. This is the place where Moomy was when she wasn't feeling good. The place with all the strange smells, loud noises, and people who wouldn't let me go inside last time. Are we going back in? I wonder, feeling a bit confused. Last time, I had to stay in the box. But today, things feel different.

We all get out of the big box, and my paws hit the ground with a little bounce. I look around, recognizing the place but unsure what's going to happen next. I follow Missy, Moomy, and Daard as we walk toward the big opening, the one where I had to stop last time.

That's when I saw her—the same hooman who had sent me back to the box before. I remember her. She smells the same. Last time, she didn't let me in, but this time, Moomy softly barks something to her, and the hooman smiles as she looks down at me. My tail wags slowly. She kneels and strokes my head, and I still don't fully understand what's happening, but she seems different today. She barks something I don't quite catch, then looks up at Missy, who is standing beside me with her hand resting on my back.

The hooman and Missy shake paws—I've seen hoomans do that before—and then she steps aside. *Wait... she's letting us in!* I look up at Missy, who gives me a soft smile, and I realise that this time, I'm allowed to go with them.

We walk through the big opening, and the smells hit me all at once—the same smells from before medicine, people, and something that reminds me of when Moomy was feeling unwell. But this time, I'm not confused or worried. Missy's hand is steady on my lead, and I'm ready. I have my bright yellow jacket, and I remember what this means now. *I'm here to help.*

Inside, there are people everywhere. Some look tired, some seem a little sad, but I keep my eyes on Missy, waiting for what she wants me to do. As we walk down the long hallways, I notice some children, smaller hoomans, pointing at me and smiling. One little girl is sitting on a big bed with wheels, and when she sees me, her eyes light up. She waves, and I wag my tail back at her, knowing that I'm here to make people feel better.

Missy stops walking, and I sit down next to her, just like I've been trained to do. I look up at her, waiting for her command. She kneels beside me, giving me a pat on the head. "Good boy, Rex," she whispers, her voice a little less shaky now.

We move toward a group of people, and I can see they're watching me. One of them, a lady with a soft voice, reaches out her hand to me. Missy gently loosens the line and lets me step forward. I walk up to the lady and sit down in front of her. She reaches out and strokes my fur, and I can feel the softness in her touch like she's been waiting for this moment. I stay calm, just like I've been trained, letting her pet me.

I hear the hoomans talking to each other, their voices quieter now. Moomy is nearby, smiling as she watches me interact with the people. I remember how I used to sit next to her when she was feeling weak and tired, how I would lay my head in her lap and make her feel better. Now, I get to do the same for these people. It's a strange new feeling, but it feels good.

As we leave the room, Missy is smiling. I can tell she's proud of me, and I feel a little proud too. I still don't understand everything that's going on, but I know that I'm doing something important. And that's enough for me.

Chapter 10

Rex's Next Visit: Comforting the Kind-Eyed Man

A few sleeps later, we went to a new place. This one felt different—quieter, slower. When we walked in, I saw lots of older hoomans sitting around in chairs. Some of them were sleeping, others were eating. I could tell right away that this wasn't like the hospital or the places where children played. It felt calmer here like time was moving a little slower. I stayed close to Missy, walking quietly by her side.

As we entered the room, I noticed one hooman waving to Missy, so we went over to him. He was an older man, sitting in a chair, and he looked a little confused. He didn't bark like most hoomans do; instead, he made a sound—*argh*—and I wasn't sure what it meant. Missy spoke to another hooman nearby, and I caught a word I didn't understand—something like *non-verbal*. I'm not sure if I heard it right, but it didn't matter much to me. I was focused on the man in front of me, the one with kind eyes.

He looked a bit lost, like he didn't know what to do. I wasn't sure what to do either, but I remembered what I did for Moomy when she wasn't feeling well. So, I did what felt right—I put my head in his lap, gently resting it there, just like I did with Moomy.

For a moment, the man just stared at me, his kind eyes a little wide, like he didn't expect me to do that. Then, slowly, he reached out and placed his hand—on my head. He smiled, and though he didn't say much, I could feel the warmth in his touch. He made that *argh* sound again, but this time it was softer, gentler, like it meant something good. His mouth lifted into a smile, and I wagged my tail just a little, happy that I made him feel better.

Missy was standing nearby and softly said, "His name is Rex." I think she was telling him my name, but the man didn't say anything back. He just kept stroking my head, and I could feel how much that simple touch meant to him. We stayed like that for a little while before Missy gently moved us on to visit the other hoomans in the room.

Most of the other hoomans were happy to see me, smiling and reaching out to pet me as we made our way around the room. But there was one man who didn't want to say hello. When I came near, he lifted his paw and barked, "No!" Missy understood right away and moved us away without hesitation. Not everyone wants to meet me, and that's okay. I know Missy will always guide me where I'm needed most.

After what felt like a short visit, we left. I had a good feeling about the day, but it wasn't long before we came back again. This time, I recognised the room right away, and the hoomans who were sitting there the last time were still in their chairs. I was eager to see if the kind-eyed man was here, too.

And then I saw him. He was sitting in a chair by the opening that led to the big green area outside. I pulled a little on my lead, wanting to go see him, but Missy held me back for a moment. I looked up at her, and she seemed to understand what I wanted, so she let me go.

I walked over to the kind-eyed man, and when he saw me, his face lit up. He reached out his hand toward me and softly said, "Weeeex." That's me! He was trying to say my name. As soon as I heard him, I knew I had to get closer. I put my head in his lap again, just like before, and I could feel how calm he became almost immediately.

Everyone around us had gone quiet. It was strange, really. Usually, there's always some noise, but not today. The room was silent, except for the sound of the kind-eyed man softly repeating, "Weeeex." Missy was standing nearby, quietly talking to a younger hooman who was watching the man closely. I could feel the calm energy in the room, and even though I didn't understand the quiet, I knew this was an important moment.

The man kept stroking my head and then down my back, over and over, his hand moving gently, as if he was trying to memorise how I felt. He seemed so happy, so peaceful, and I could feel that my presence was making a difference. His smile grew a little wider, and he said the sound again, "Weeeex." Each time he said it, I felt the quiet in the room deepen, like everyone was watching this moment unfold, but no one wanted to interrupt it.

I don't understand everything about what happened that day, but I do know that I made the kind-eyed man happy. And that's enough for me.

A Good Night's Sleep

That night, I slept so well. There was a warmth in my chest that felt different from other days. I knew Missy and I had done well. She couldn't hide her excitement the whole way home, and she kept repeating those words— "Good boy." I hear them a lot, but today they felt extra special. The way she said them, with that proud tone in her voice, made me feel like I'd done something really important. I didn't do much—just what I was trained to do—but something about it felt bigger.

I kept thinking about the man with the kind eyes, the way he smiled when I put my head in his lap. I hadn't seen him say much, but there was something about the way he looked at me that made me feel very close to him. When he said my name, even in that soft, drawn-out way, "Weeeex," I could tell I had helped him in some way I didn't fully understand.

Missy was so happy with what happened. I could feel her excitement buzzing the whole time we were together, and that made me happy too. We were a team, and today, we'd done something that made a real difference. It wasn't like playing in the park or running with other dogs—this was quieter, deeper.

As I drifted off to sleep, curled up in my usual spot, I felt good knowing I'd done what I was trained to do. But it was more than just following commands. I felt a connection with that man, and somehow, I knew I'd be seeing him again. Even though I didn't fully understand what had happened, I knew one thing—Missy was proud of me, and I'd made a difference. That's all I needed to know.

And as I slept, I dreamed of kind eyes and gentle pats on the head, feeling closer to my family and the people I was meant to help.

Another Visit with the Kind-Eyed Man

A few more sleeps passed, and I found myself back in the big moving box with Missy and Daard. I've come to understand that these trips aren't just about me anymore. It's about the people we're visiting—the people who need a bit of comfort, a smile, or just someone to sit quietly with them for a while.

Missy seems calmer this time and more confident. Her hands don't shake like they used to when she's putting on my bright yellow back cover with *Pets As Therapy* written across it. She's getting as good as Shaarly was at this whole training thing. I'm proud of her. I can tell she's proud of me, too, and that makes me feel like a very good boy.

We arrive at the same quiet place with the older hoomans sitting in their chairs. I recognise the scent of the room, the slower pace of everything, and the soft sounds of hooman voices. I know what to do now—I walk calmly beside Missy, my lead loose and comfortable, feeling ready for the day ahead.

As soon as we walk in, I start looking around for the kind-eyed man. I wonder if he's here today. He had such a gentle way about him, and I felt a strong connection with him the last time we met. I hope I can see him again, just to rest my head in his lap like I did before.

Missy greets some of the other hoomans, who smile and wave at me. I give a soft wag of my tail in return, but I'm still scanning the room, searching. And then I see him—sitting in his chair by the window, looking out into the big green area outside. He hasn't noticed us yet, but as soon as we move closer, I see a flicker of recognition in his eyes.

Missy seems to know where I want to go. She gives me a soft smile and gently lets me lead the way, holding onto my lead but trusting me to move toward him.

When we reach the kind-eyed man, he looks down at me and his face softens into a smile, just like the last time. His hand trembles a little as he reaches out to me, and I feel that same warmth inside me as I place my head in his lap, just like before. He gently strokes my head, his touch shaky but filled with tenderness.

He barks that soft sound again, "Weeeex." Hearing him say my name makes me wag my tail a little more, but I stay calm, knowing that my presence is what's important here. I can feel him relax as he continues to stroke my fur, his hand moving from my head to my back. It's like he's remembering me, even though we don't speak the same language.

Missy is standing nearby, talking softly to a younger hooman. They're both watching the kind-eyed man closely, and I notice something different today. The room is quieter, just like the last time. No one is making a lot of noise, but there's a sense of calm in the air. The kind-eyed man's breathing slows as he continues to pet me, and I can see the happiness in his eyes, even though he doesn't say much.

I stay with him for a while, just being there, my head resting on his legs. Every now and then, he makes that soft sound again—"Weeeex"—and each time, it feels like a little piece of him is waking up. I don't know why, but it makes me happy, too.

Eventually, Missy gently tugs on my lead, signalling that it's time to move on. I look up at the kind-eyed man one last time before we go, and he gives me a small smile. His hand lingers on my head for just a moment longer, and I feel that connection again. It's hard to explain, but I know I've made a difference, even if all I did was sit with him.

As we leave, I glance back at him. He's still watching me, and for the first time, I see a bit of light in his eyes that wasn't there before. I feel proud again, knowing that I've helped in some small way.

Reflections on the Visit

As we get back into the big box and head home, Missy is quieter than usual. I can tell she's thinking about what just happened, her eyes soft and thoughtful. She reaches down and pats my head gently, whispering, "Good boy, Rex."

I can feel her pride and emotion, and even though I don't fully understand everything, I know that today was special, not just for me but for the kind-eyed man. I think I'll be seeing him again soon.

Charlie's Special Visitor

A few sleeps have passed, and things have been mostly the same—morning walks, visits to the care home, and lots of time with Missy and Daard. But today, something feels a little different. There's a sense of excitement around the house, and I can hear the family talking a lot about Charlie. I haven't seen him as much lately, but whenever he's home, it's always a fun time.

Today, though, the excitement isn't just about Charlie coming home. It's about someone else. There's another scent in the house—one I don't recognise—a new hooman scent.

When Charlie walks through the door, I can already feel my tail wagging. I haven't seen him in what feels like forever, and just having him home again makes me want to run up and greet him. But wait—there's someone with him! A new face. A girl, hooman, is smiling brightly and laughing as she talks with Charlie.

I look up at Missy, who seems just as excited as me. She leans down and whispers, "Guess what, Rex? This is Charlie's girlfriend, and she's been dying to meet you!"

Girlfriend? That's a new word. I don't know what it means exactly, but from the way everyone's acting, it seems like this is an important visitor. The new hooman—Charlie's girlfriend—looks at me with the biggest smile on her face. I can tell she's excited to meet me too. Her eyes light up when she sees me, and her hands clap together with joy.

"Oh my gosh! This is Rex?" she says, her voice full of excitement as she crouches down to my level. "I've heard so much about you!"

Charlie laughs and nods, watching as his girlfriend reaches out to pet me. Her hand is soft, and I can tell right away that she's a nice hooman. She smells good too—like fresh flowers and something sweet. I like her already. My tail starts wagging even faster as I walk up to her, letting her scratch behind my ears.

"You're even cuter than Charlie said," she says with a laugh, rubbing my head gently. "He talks about you all the time, you know?"

I glance up at Charlie, and he's smiling too. I can see how much he likes her. The way they look at each other, the way they laugh together—it feels good to see him so happy. And I'm happy too, especially because this new hooman is giving me so much attention!

Charlie's girlfriend spends a long time petting me, her hands moving gently along my back and scratching in all the right spots. I roll onto my side, enjoying the attention, and she laughs again, clearly delighted by my response.

"I've always wanted to meet you, Rex," she says softly, still stroking my fur. "Charlie told me how special you are, especially with everything you've done for the family."

I'm not sure what she means, but I can tell she's happy to be here, and I'm glad to have made a new friend. My tail hasn't stopped wagging since she walked through the door, and I don't think it's going to stop anytime soon.

Chapter 11

The Family's Reactions

As the day goes on, the house is filled with laughter and smiles. Shaarly, his girlfriend, Missy, and Daard all gather around, talking and enjoying each other's company. I stay close, moving between them, soaking in the happy energy. Charlie's girlfriend keeps looking over at me, giving me extra pats and smiles, and I can tell she's already part of the family.

Later, I overhear Missy talking to Shaarly. "She's great, Shaarly. I love how much she loves Rex already."

Shaarly smiles, glancing over at me. "Yeah, she couldn't wait to meet him. She kept asking when she'd finally get to come over."

I feel proud hearing them talk about me like that. It feels good to know that even someone new to the family already loves me. I know this is the start of something special.

A Seaside Holiday in Cornwall, England: Through Rex's Eyes

It all started with the rustling of bags and the sounds of excitement. I could tell something was happening—something big. Missy and Shaarly were running around the house, putting things into bags and boxes, while Daard was moving things into the big box with wheels outside. I knew this feeling. We were going somewhere. And I was going too.

Missy came over to me, her face full of excitement, and clipped my lead onto my collar. "Ready, Rex?" she asked, smiling down at me. I wagged my tail as hard as I could. I didn't know where we were going, but I was definitely ready.

We all piled into the big moving box, and I found my spot in the back seat between Missy and Charlie.

Moomy and Daard were in the front, talking about something called *Cornwall*. I wasn't sure what Cornwall was, but if it involved a lot of hooman excitement, then I knew it was going to be good.

The Long Drive and the First Sniffs of Cornwall

The drive was long, and after a while, I settled down for a nap. I felt the box rumbling beneath me and the occasional stops where I got to stretch my legs and sniff around unfamiliar places. Every time we stopped, there were new smells—different dogs had been there, strange plants, and the salty smell of something I couldn't quite place yet.

Finally, after what felt like ages, we stopped for good. The doors opened, and I jumped out, my nose twitching with excitement. The air was different here. It was fresh and salty, with a breeze that ruffled my fur. I liked it already.

We had arrived at a place called a *cottage*. I wasn't sure what that meant, but it had a big green area just for me! I ran around, exploring every corner while Missy and Shaarly unpacked the bags. There was a small fence so that I couldn't run too far, but that was okay—there was so much to sniff right here.

Day 1: The Beach and the Strange Moving Water

The next morning, we set off on a new adventure. Moomy, Daard, Missy, and Shaarly all seemed excited as they put my lead on, and we walked down a sandy path. The wind carried a scent I'd never smelled before—strong and salty. It made my nose twitch with curiosity.

When we reached the end of the path, my paws hit something soft and strange. It wasn't like the ground at home—this was... squishy, and it moved under my feet. I recognise this from before - Sand. Missy giggled as I lifted my paw to inspect it, but I quickly got used to the feeling again. There was so much to explore here, and I could hear something roaring in the distance.

As we moved closer, I saw it—the sea again. .It was big and wide and kept moving, rushing up toward me and then pulling away again. I looked at Missy and Shaarly for reassurance, and they just laughed. Shaarly ran ahead, calling my name, and dashed right into the water.

I wasn't so sure about that. The water looked... tricky. But Shaarly called me again, and my legs started moving before I could think about it. Slowly at first, I paddled toward the edge, sniffing cautiously as the water came up to greet me. I jumped back when it touched my paws—it was cool and a little scary at first.

But then Charlie laughed and splashed around, and I could see that it was safe. So, I took a deep breath, and before I knew it, I was running right into the waves, splashing alongside Shaarly. The water was fun! It moved and played back, and I could chase it as it pulled away from the shore.

Missy threw a ball, and I bounded after it, splashing through the shallow waves, feeling the cool water on my paws. I barked happily, running back to her, the salty water dripping from my fur. This place was amazing!

Day 2: Coastal Walks and the Smell of Adventure

The next day, we went on a long walk along a high path that overlooked the sea. The ground beneath my paws was rough, and the wind was strong, carrying all sorts of new smells up from the cliffs below.

We passed through small living places with narrow streets, where people smiled at me and patted my head as we walked by. Every so often, we would stop at a small shop, and I'd get fresh water and a treat while the hoomans ate strange-smelling things they called pasties.

I liked the walks a lot. They were full of new places to explore, and Missy and Charlie took turns holding my lead, pointing out things for me to see—even though I was more interested in the smells.

Day 3: The Boat and My First Ice Cream

That day, we did something really different. The hoomans took me onto something called a boat. At first, I wasn't sure about it—it moved in a way I wasn't used to, rocking gently beneath my paws. But after a little while, I realised it wasn't so bad. The wind was in my fur, and I could see the sea all around us. The smell of the salt and the ocean was everywhere, and it was kind of exciting to be out in the middle of it all.

After the boat ride, we stopped at a small stand where Moomy and Daard got something cold and sweet-smelling. Missy came over to me with a special surprise—a small bowl with something inside. She called it dog-friendly ice cream. I wasn't sure at first, but once I took a lick, I knew I loved it! It was cold, creamy, and delicious, and I wagged my tail the whole time I ate it.

Day 4: Exploring the Gardens

On another day, we visited a place with lots of flowers and trees. It was called a garden, but it wasn't like the small one at the cottage—this one was huge, with winding paths and strange, colourful plants. The smells were incredible—so many different scents all at once! I could have spent the whole day sniffing, but the hoomans wanted to keep moving, so I followed them as they explored the garden.

Missy and Shaarly took pictures of me in front of the flowers, and I tried to sit still, even though I was itching to run off and explore. There were birds everywhere, and I wanted to chase them, but I stayed calm, just like I was trained to do. The hoomans were happy, and that made me happy, too.

Day 5: One Last Day on the Beach

Our last day was spent back at the beach. By now, I knew the routine—run, chase the waves, fetch the ball, and roll in the sand. It was perfect.

Missy and Shaarly laughed as I ran back and forth, kicking up sand behind me. I splashed in the shallow water, my paws sinking into the wet sand as I chased after the ball. The sun was bright, and everything smelled fresh and salty.

As the day ended, we sat together on the beach, watching the sun dip into the horizon. I lay down beside Missy, my fur still damp from the sea, and she scratched behind my ears in that perfect spot. The hoomans were quiet, just watching the waves, and I closed my eyes, feeling the warmth of the day settle in.

Heading Home

The next day, we packed up the big box again. I watched as the hoomans loaded everything back in, my tail wagging even though I was a little sad to leave. It had been full of new smells, new places, and lots of fun. I didn't know when we'd be back, but I knew one thing: wherever my family went, I would go too. And that was all that mattered.

As we drove away, I lay down in the backseat, tired but happy, dreaming of the sea, the sand, and all the adventures we had shared.

Rex Visits a School: Listening to Children Read (with Missy and Shaarly)

It was another one of those days. I could feel it the moment Missy put on my yellow *Pets As Therapy* jacket and clipped on my collar. Something special was happening, but today felt a bit different. There was extra energy in the air and more movement around the house. I noticed Shaarly was coming with us this time, too. It wasn't just going to be me and Missy—Shaarly had a serious look on his face, like he was thinking about something important. I wasn't sure what it all meant, but I knew I was ready for whatever the day had in store.

As we got into the big moving box, I could hear Missy and Shaarly talking excitedly. There was that word again, school. Missy had said it before, but today, Shaarly seemed extra interested. I listened to them as we drove, curious about what this visit would be like.

"I've been reading about this new scheme," Shaarly said. "Kids who have trouble reading get more confident if they read to dogs. It's because dogs don't judge or criticise them—they can just practice without fear."

Missy nodded enthusiastically. "Yeah! And Rex is the perfect dog for it. He's so calm and patient. I think the kids will love reading to him."

I didn't understand all of their words, but I heard calm, and I knew what that meant. It was something I'd practised a lot with Missy and Shaarly. When I was calm, everyone was happy.

The School Visit: A New Experience with Shaarly and Missy

When we arrived, I could already hear the sounds of excited voices. It was the same school as before, with bright walls and lots of little hoomans running around. Their laughter filled the air, and I could feel my tail wagging as we walked inside.

This time, though, Shaarly was with us. I was used to Missy handling me during these visits, but today, it felt like Shaarly was taking a closer look at everything. He was watching how the children moved, how they interacted with the teachers, and how I reacted to the new environment. I wasn't sure what he was thinking about, but I could tell he was interested.

The teacher welcomed us warmly. "Ah, you brought Rex again! The children were so excited to read to him last time," she said, smiling down at me. "And I see you brought someone new," she added, looking at Shaarly.

Shaarly introduced himself and explained why he was there. "I've been reading about how dogs can help children with reading difficulties," he said. "I wanted to see it in action and learn more. I'm really interested in how this program works."

The teacher nodded, understanding. "It's a wonderful idea. The children feel so much more relaxed when they're reading to Rex. There's no pressure, no judgment—just a friendly face to listen. We've seen real improvement."

Shaarly seemed to like that answer, and I could see him thinking hard, probably about how he could help make this work for more children.

Listening to the Children Read

We walked into a colourful classroom where the children were already waiting, their books in hand. They had big smiles on their faces when they saw me, and some of them waved excitedly. I liked seeing them so happy—it made my tail wag even faster.

Missy guided me to a soft spot on the floor, and I sat down like I'd been taught. One by one, the children came over with their books, ready to read. The first child was a little boy who looked a bit nervous. His hands were shaking slightly as he held his book, and I could feel his uncertainty.

Missy smiled at him gently. "Don't worry, Rex is here to listen. He loves hearing stories, and he's really good at it."

The boy looked at me, his eyes wide, but after a moment, he knelt in front of me and opened his book. His voice was quiet at first, stumbling over some of the words, but I stayed still, my head tilting slightly as I listened. I didn't need to understand the words to know that he was trying his best.

Slowly, the boy's voice grew steadier. He glanced at me now and then, and each time, I wagged my tail a little to show him that I was listening. As he read, I noticed that his shoulders relaxed, and by the time he finished the story, he was smiling.

Shaarly, who had been watching closely, nodded approvingly. "That's amazing," he said softly to Missy. "You can really see how Rex helps take the pressure off. The boy started so unsure, but by the end, he was confident."

Missy smiled. "Rex just listens. That's all the kids need sometimes—someone who listens without judging."

The Scheme: Helping Children with Reading Difficulties

As the session continued, more children took their turns reading to me. Some were shy, others more confident, but all of them seemed to enjoy sitting with me and sharing their stories. I loved the way their faces lit up when they realised I wasn't going to correct them or laugh if they made a mistake. I was just there to listen—and I was happy to do it.

Shaarly stayed close, watching how the children interacted with me. After a while, he spoke quietly to the teacher. "I think this scheme could really make a difference for a lot of kids. If more schools had dogs like Rex, I think children who struggle with reading would have a much easier time."

The teacher nodded. "Absolutely. We've already seen improvements in the children who read to Rex. They're more willing to try, and their confidence grows with each session."

I didn't understand all the words they were saying, but I could feel the pride in the room. Missy was smiling, and Shaarly looked like he was thinking hard about something. I had a feeling that this was the start of something bigger—something that might help even more children.

A Special Moment with One Child

Near the end of the session, a little girl who hadn't spoken much all morning came up to me. She looked very shy, her eyes downcast as she clutched her book to her chest. Missy smiled at her and patted my head. "Rex would love to hear your story," she said softly.

The girl hesitated for a moment, then slowly sat down next to me. She opened her book, her hands trembling slightly, and began to read. Her voice was barely a whisper at first, and I could feel her nerves. I leaned closer, resting my head on her lap, hoping to make her feel better.

As she continued, her voice grew a little louder. I stayed still, my ears twitching as I listened, and now and then, I wagged my tail to show her I was paying attention. Slowly but surely, she relaxed. Her words became clearer, and by the time she finished, there was a tiny smile on her face.

The teacher, Missy, and Shaarly all smiled at each other. Shaarly whispered to the teacher, "That's exactly what I've been reading about. It's incredible how much Rex helps with their confidence."

Leaving the School with a New Idea

As we left the school that day, I could tell Shaarly was excited about something. "I'm really going to look into this more," he said to Missy. "I think this reading scheme could be a game-changer for kids who struggle with reading. Rex is amazing with them, and if other dogs could do the same, it could help so many children."

Missy nodded, beaming with pride. "Yeah, I think Rex really loves it too."

I wagged my tail, happy to have made so many new friends today. I didn't fully understand everything, but I knew one thing—I loved listening to the children read. It made them happy, and that made me happy too.

Chapter 12

A Day Out at the Summer Fair: Meeting Other Therapy Dogs and Their Owners

Today was no ordinary day. As soon as Missy put on my yellow *Pets As Therapy* jacket and clipped on my collar, I could feel the excitement buzzing through her. Daard and Moomy were coming too, and everyone was talking about something called a *Summer Fair*. I didn't know exactly what that meant, but if Missy was this happy, I knew it was going to be something special.

After a short drive, we arrived at a big, open field. Bright colours, loud laughter, and delicious smells filled the air. There were stalls everywhere with food, games, and people walking around with wide smiles and happy voices. But the best part? There were other dogs—dogs who looked just like me in their own therapy jackets, each one walking beside their hooman with a calm, friendly expression.

As we walked through the fair, we were greeted by an older lady with a Golden Retriever named Bailey. Bailey had the same yellow jacket as me and seemed just as calm. She looked at me with kind eyes, her tail wagging gently. I wagged mine back, sniffing the air between us in a polite hello.

"Is this your dog?" the lady asked Missy, sounding surprised.

"Yes! I'm Rex's handler," Missy replied proudly, her hand resting on my head.

The lady looked impressed. "A young handler! That's wonderful. You don't see many young people working as therapy dog handlers. It's usually us older folks," she said with a laugh. Her Golden Retriever, Bailey, gave me a friendly nudge with her nose, and I nudged her back, liking her immediately.

Meeting Other Therapy Dogs

As we walked around the fair, we met more therapy dogs with their handlers. There was Max, a big

German Shepherd with soft eyes and a gentle demeanour; Daisy, a small, fluffy Shih Tzu who pranced around with a joyful bounce; and Bruno, a calm Labrador who looked as though he had seen it all. All the dogs wore the same yellow jacket, and all of them had the same calm, patient look that I had come to know as part of being a therapy dog.

Each hooman we met seemed surprised to see Missy, a teenager, handling me so confidently. They'd ask her questions, curious about how she got started with therapy work. Missy explained that I'd been helping our family and friends for a while and that we'd trained together for therapy visits. I could see how proud she was, and that made me proud too.

One man with a gentle Border Collie named Lucy leaned down to pat my head. "You're very lucky to have such a young, dedicated handler, Rex," he said kindly. Lucy, his Border Collie, wagged her tail at me, her eyes shining with warmth. I wagged my tail back, and we sniffed noses, happy to meet another friend with the same calmness that we shared.

A Group of New Friends

At one point, all the therapy dogs and their handlers gathered in a shady area of the fair. Each dog sat calmly by their hooman's side, watching as people walked by, some stopping to say hello or pat us. There were children and adults, all curious about our work as therapy dogs, and Missy and the other hoomans explained what we did, sharing stories of how we helped bring comfort to those who needed it.

The older handlers watched Missy with interest, impressed by her calm confidence. "It's wonderful to see a young person doing this," one lady said, her voice kind and encouraging. "You're setting such a good example."

Missy beamed, giving me a quick scratch behind the ears. "Thank you. I love doing this with Rex. He's my partner," she said, smiling down at me.

As we sat with the group, I could feel the shared energy between all the dogs. Each of us was different in size, breed, and colour, but we all had the same purpose — to bring calm, comfort, and happiness to those we met. Bailey, the Golden Retriever, lay down beside me, her head resting on her paws. "It's good to meet another one of us," she seemed to say with a slow wag of her tail.

A Walk Through the Fair

After the group meeting, Missy and I walked around the fair, stopping by various stalls where we met other people who wanted to know more about our therapy work. I stayed close to Missy, keeping my steps slow and calm, just like I had been taught.

We passed a stall where someone was making candy floss, and the sweet smell filled the air, making my nose twitch with curiosity. A little girl came up and asked if she could pet me, and with Missy's permission, I sat still while the girl gently stroked my head. I could see her smile grow as she patted my fur, and I wagged my tail to show her I was happy too.

Missy chatted with her parents, explaining that I was a therapy dog. "Rex listens to children read, and he visits places where people need comfort," she said. The parents looked impressed, and the girl giggled, hugging me gently before skipping back to her family.

The Therapy Dog Show-and-Tell

One of the fair's main events was a "Show-and-Tell" for therapy dogs, where each handler got to introduce their dog and explain what we did. Missy and I waited our turn, watching as each dog took centre stage with their handler.

When it was our turn, Missy and I walked out together, and she introduced me to the crowd. "This is Rex, and he's a therapy dog," she said confidently. "He visits schools to listen to children read, and he also goes to care homes where he brings comfort to people who need a friendly face."

I sat beside her, my tail wagging as I looked out at the crowd. There were so many smiling faces, and I could feel the warmth and curiosity in the air. Missy talked about how much she loved working with me and how proud she was of everything we had learned together. The crowd clapped, and I could feel the pride in her voice. It made me want to do my best, always.

A Shared Understanding

After the show, we gathered with the other therapy dogs and their handlers one last time. There was a quiet understanding between us, a bond that went beyond words. Each dog was different—a big German Shepherd, a tiny Shih Tzu, a calm Labrador, and so many others. But despite our differences, we all shared the same purpose.

The older hoomans patted Missy's shoulder, offering her kind words and encouragement. "You're a natural, Missy," one woman said. "It's so wonderful to see young people getting involved in therapy work."

Missy smiled, glancing down at me. "Rex has taught me so much. We are a team."

I wagged my tail, feeling the truth in her words. This was more than just a visit or a fair—it was a reminder of the work we did together, of the calm and joy we brought to people. I was proud to be by Missy's side, proud to be a part of this group, and proud to know that even though we were different, we all shared the same purpose.

As the sun started to set, we said our goodbyes, exchanging wags and soft nudges with the other dogs. I knew we'd go back to our therapy visits soon, but today had been special. I had met new friends, seen new things, and felt the joy of being part of something bigger.

On the way home, Missy scratched behind my ears, her face glowing with happiness. "You were amazing today, Rex," she whispered. And in that moment, I knew there was no place I'd rather be than right here, with my family, doing what I loved most.

A Restful Few Years: Rex's Life of Service and Family Joy

For the next couple of years, life settled into a peaceful, joyful rhythm. I continued to visit schools, hospitals, and care homes with Missy by my side. We had become a team, bringing smiles, comfort, and calm wherever we went. Each place had its own sounds and smells, and I'd learned to tell when someone needed a little extra time with me—whether it was a child learning to read, an older hooman in a hospital room, or a resident in a care home who just wanted to rest their hand on my fur.

Missy was growing up, but she still looked at me with the same proud smile she'd had from the start. We'd built a routine that felt familiar and warm. Our therapy visits were filled with soft voices and gentle pats, with people saying "thank you" to Missy and me, even though I felt I was just doing what came naturally.

Then, in between our work, there were holidays. Every so often, Daard, Moomy, Missy, and sometimes even Shaarly, would pack up the Big Box, and we'd head out to new places. We explored different beaches, stayed in cosy cottages, and wandered through fields filled with strange and wonderful scents. These times were filled with laughter and calm, with Moomy's gentle smiles and Daard's steady hand on my head, scratching behind my ears as we watched the sunset.

Shaarly's Wedding

One day, the house was busier than usual, and I could feel the excitement in the air. Missy was getting dressed in a beautiful outfit, and Moomy was fixing her hair in front of a mirror. Daard was wearing a suit, and even Shaarly, who usually dressed casually, looked very smart. The house was buzzing, and I couldn't help but wag my tail, feeding off everyone's excitement.

"Ready, Rex?" Missy said, kneeling to clip on my lead. "You're coming with us today. Shaarly's getting married, and he wants you there."

I didn't know what *married* meant, but I understood that today was important. We drove to a place filled with flowers, lights, and lots of people. When I arrived, I was greeted by Shaarly, who gave me a big smile and a scratch behind my ears. He looked happy, and I could tell that this day was something special for him.

The ceremony was calm and quiet, with gentle music and soft voices. I sat next to Missy, staying as still as I could. Afterwards, we went to a place filled with laughter and more people, and I realised this was what they called a *reception*. There was a lot of food, and I kept getting little treats from people who passed by. Everyone seemed to want to pet me and tell me how "good" and "handsome" I was, which I didn't mind at all.

Shaarly even danced with his new wife, and every so often, he'd look over at me with a smile as if to say, "Thank you for being here." I felt proud to be part of his special day, happy to see him smiling and surrounded by family.

The Years Pass and Change Comes

The Years Pass and Change Comes

Time passed, filled with the routines of our visits and the warmth of family moments. I continued to visit the schools, homes, and hospitals where I'd come to know so many friendly faces. Missy still guided me on each visit, her confidence growing even stronger with each passing year. Every so often, people would ask her if I was getting older, and she'd smile and say, "Maybe, but he's still got plenty of energy."

But then, one morning, I woke up and felt different. Something was wrong. My world felt like it was spinning, even though I was standing still. When I tried to move, my paws didn't take me where I expected, and I stumbled. The room felt tilted, and I couldn't understand why.

Missy noticed right away. "Rex, what's wrong?" she asked, her voice filled with worry. She put her arms around me, trying to steady me, but I could tell she was frightened.

Daard and Moomy rushed over, and before I knew it, we were back in the big moving box, heading to a place I recognised—the vet's office. The smells and sounds here were familiar, but today, they felt overwhelming. My world was spinning, and I didn't know why.

At the vet, the hoomans talked in soft voices, and Missy kept her hand on my head, stroking my fur gently. The vet examined me, speaking softly as she looked into my eyes and checked my movements.

After a while, she explained something to Missy and the family. "Rex has vestibular disease," she said gently. "It affects his balance, which is why he feels unsteady. There's no specific cure, but with time and supportive care, he should improve on his own."

Missy's face softened a little as she listened. "So he'll get better?" she asked, her voice hopeful.

The vet nodded. "Most dogs do. He'll need some help—keeping him in a safe space, gentle physiotherapy, and just taking things slow. But with care, he should be back to himself soon."

Chapter 13

A New Chapter: Healing at Home

Back at home, things were different. I was tired more often, and moving felt strange. Missy and Moomy set up a comfortable area for me with soft blankets and familiar toys. Missy would sit beside me, her gentle hands helping me when I felt unsteady. She was careful with me, watching over me like she had from the beginning, her quiet strength keeping me calm.

There were days when I'd feel frustrated when my paws didn't seem to want to take me where I wanted to go. But Missy and Daard were patient, always there to steady me. They encouraged me to take slow, careful steps, and each time I succeeded, I could see the pride in their eyes. It was as if they were saying, "You're doing great, Rex. Just keep trying."

As the weeks passed, I began to feel a little better. The world didn't spin as much, and I was able to take more steps on my own. Missy would smile and say "Good boy" in that soft, reassuring voice that always made me feel safe.

The Love of Family and a New Pace

Life had slowed down, but I felt the love of my family even more. There were fewer therapy visits now, but I didn't mind. Instead, I found joy in the smaller things—Missy's gentle hands guiding me, Daard's calm presence by my side, and Moomy's quiet smiles when I managed to walk across the room on my own.

Even Shaarly visited often, sometimes with his wife, who'd become part of our family too. They would sit with me, talking softly and reminding me of all the happy memories we'd shared. I was surrounded by love, patience, and warmth.

As my world settled back into balance, I realised that I didn't need to be the energetic dog I once was. My family loved me for who I was, and I was grateful for every moment I spent with them.

Reflections on the Journey

As the days passed, I grew stronger. Each day felt like a gift, a reminder of the wonderful life I'd shared with my family. There were fewer therapy visits, but now and then, we'd visit a familiar place, bringing comfort to the people who'd come to know me over the years.

Even though I couldn't run or play the way I used to, I found joy in the simple moments—a pat from Daard, a smile from Missy, a quiet evening with Moomy by my side. And as I looked at the faces of the people I loved, I knew one thing: my family had given me a life full of love, and I had given them the same in return. That was all I could ever ask for.

In the end, my world wasn't perfect, but it was filled with love and gratitude. And as I lay down beside Missy, her hand resting gently on my back, I knew that I was exactly where I belonged.

It was a quiet morning when Shaarly and his wife arrived at the house, their faces bright with smiles. I was resting in my favourite spot on the soft blanket Missy had set up for me, feeling comfortable and warm. But as soon as I saw Shaarly, my tail gave a little wag. Even though I wasn't as energetic as before, the sight of him always made me happy.

Shaarly knelt beside me, scratching that perfect spot behind my ears. "Hey, Rex," he said softly, his voice warm. "We brought you a special treat."

His wife leaned down and opened a small box, revealing the most amazing thing I'd ever seen. It was a doggie cake, specially made just for me, topped with treats and smelling like all my favourite flavours. I gave it a big sniff, and Shaarly laughed, holding it up for me to see.

"Only the best for you, buddy," he said. Carefully, they cut a small piece, and I got to enjoy my special treat right there with everyone watching and smiling.

As I chewed happily, Missy and Moomy's faces were full of excitement and warmth. Shaarly cleared his throat, glancing at his wife, who smiled and took his hand.

"We actually have some news, too," he said, his voice a little softer. "In about seven months, we're expecting… a baby."

There was a beat of silence, and then Missy's face lit up with pure joy. She clapped her hands over her mouth, her eyes already filling with tears. "A baby? I'm going to be an aunt?" she cried, her voice breaking with happiness.

Shaarly laughed, giving her a big hug as she wiped her happy tears. "Yes, Missy. You're going to be an aunt."

Even though I didn't understand every word, I could feel the excitement and joy in the room. Shaarly patted my head again, his hand gentle. "Looks like you'll have a new little friend soon, Rex," he said with a smile.

I didn't know what the future held, but with the happiness around me, I knew one thing—I had a family who loved me, and soon, there'd be even more love to go around. And as I lay there, content and surrounded by my family, I felt warm and peaceful, ready to welcome whatever came next.

As the days went by, I started to feel more like myself again. My balance was improving, and I was able to walk steadily beside Missy on our visits. I couldn't run like I used to, but just being able to return to my familiar places—the schools, the hospitals, the care homes—made me happy. And I could tell Missy was proud, too, especially when she'd lean down and say, "Good boy, Rex. You're doing great."

One afternoon, something was pushed through the big opening to Missy from the Kennel Club. She opened it slowly, her face a mix of excitement and surprise. Inside was an invitation to attend *Crufts* in Birmingham to help demonstrate the Gold Good Citizen Award scheme.

Her eyes lit up, but there was a hint of worry there, too. She glanced over at Daard, who was watching her closely. "This… this is huge," she murmured, turning the invitation over in her hands. "They want me to show other people how the Good Citizen Scheme Award works. I'd have to speak in front of people… with Rex."

Daard smiled and put a comforting hand on her shoulder. "Yes, and that's a big honour, Missy. Think about it—there aren't many young handlers chosen for something like this. You and Rex have earned this."

Missy bit her lip, still looking uncertain. "But… what if I mess up? Or… what if I get too nervous?"

Daard led her gently to the side, his voice calm and steady. "Missy, you've worked so hard with Rex. Think of all the people you've inspired just by being a young handler in our community. This is a chance to show others that young people can make a difference with their dogs. You could encourage a whole new generation of handlers to get involved."

Missy looked at the invitation again, her face softening. "I never thought of it like that," she said, her voice a little stronger.

Daard nodded. "You're not just showing off what you've learned—you're showing what's possible. And you won't be alone; Rex will be right there with you."

She looked down at me, a small smile growing as she rubbed my head. I wagged my tail, sensing her resolve strengthening. "Okay," she whispered, more to herself than anyone else. "We'll do it together. Right, Rex?"

I didn't know what Crufts was, but I could tell it was important to Missy. And as long as we were together, I knew we could face anything that came our way.

The whole family was buzzing with excitement on the morning of our big journey to Birmingham. Everyone was there—Daard, Moomy, Shaarly, and his wife—all gathered together to support Missy and me. I could feel the energy in the air as they packed bags, double-checked tickets, and loaded everything into the big moving box. I knew this drive would be longer than usual, but I was just happy to be with everyone.

Missy seemed especially focused, her hand resting on my head every now and then as if to reassure herself. She kept glancing down at the bright pass hanging around her neck, the one from the Kennel Club. I wagged my tail to let her know I was right there beside her, ready for whatever the day would bring.

The drive was long. We stopped once on the way, giving everyone a chance to stretch, visit the toilets, and have a quick bite to eat. Missy made sure I had fresh water and a little snack, and I settled comfortably back into the car for the last part of the journey. When we finally arrived in Birmingham, the place was unlike anywhere I'd ever been. It was big and bustling, full of unfamiliar smells, voices, and sounds that made me both excited and a little nervous. But I knew this was important for Missy, so I stayed close.

When we reached the entry gate, Missy showed her special pass, while the rest of the family had to buy tickets and stay behind. She looked a little worried as she glanced back at Moomy and Daard. Moomy reached out and gave her a reassuring smile. "Don't worry, sweetheart, we'll be there watching you."

Missy's eyes softened at her words, and she nodded. "OK," she said quietly, though I could tell her nerves were still there.

As we walked forward, just the two of us now, I felt Missy's hand tighten a little on my lead. I gave her a gentle nudge with my nose, letting her know that I was with her every step of the way. She smiled down at me, taking a deep breath, and together, we moved through the busy crowds and into the heart of Crufts. I could feel her trust in me, and that made me proud.

Today would be a big day, but as long as we had each other, I knew we could do anything.

The moment we entered Crufts, I was overwhelmed by all the sights, smells, and sounds. Everywhere I looked, there were stalls full of dog treats, leads, toys, and food. Hoomans were moving around everywhere, all talking, laughing, and exploring, and so many dogs! I could smell every kind of treat imaginable, and the excitement of the crowd filled the air. Missy seemed excited too, her eyes wide as she looked at everything.

But then, a loud voice boomed through the hall, calling Missy to the Good Citizen Award Show ring. The announcement startled both of us, and Missy glanced at me with a mixture of excitement and nerves. "That's us, Rex," she said, gathering her courage. She held my lead firmly as we made our way through the crowd, quickly heading to the ring where we'd be showing everyone what we'd worked so hard on.

When we arrived, we were guided straight to the centre of the ring. I glanced around, taking in the sea of hoomans filling the stands all around us. I'd never seen so many people in one place, all eyes on us, and I could feel Missy's hand tighten slightly on the lead. But I stayed calm and steady, sensing how important it was to help her feel confident too.

A tall woman, a little bigger than Moomy, walked into the ring, and the crowd began to clap their hands together, filling the arena with loud, echoing sounds. This woman must have been someone important because everyone seemed to know her. She smiled warmly at Missy, speaking to her in a calm, friendly voice that helped Missy relax. With a deep breath, Missy answered back confidently, her voice clear despite the sea of people watching us.

The woman then asked Missy to walk me around the ring, giving everyone a demonstration of the skills we'd worked so hard to achieve for the Gold Good Citizen Award. Missy's voice was steady as she guided me, and I followed her cues carefully, making sure each step was perfect. We moved together as a team, and I could feel her trust in me with every command. Her confidence grew with each step, and I knew I couldn't let her down.

After our demonstration, Missy brought me back to the centre of the ring. She showed the crowd a few more skills we'd practised, things like staying calm and walking to heel. I felt proud, knowing I was helping Missy shine. When we finished, the crowd clapped so loudly that it filled the entire hall with noise. Missy looked at me, her face filled with relief and pride, and I gave her a gentle nuzzle in return. We'd done it.

But our time in the ring wasn't over just yet. The woman asked if anyone in the audience had questions, and several hoomans raised their hands eagerly. They wanted to know more about how Missy trained me and what it was like to work as a young handler with a therapy dog. Missy looked a little nervous as she glanced around the crowd, but she leaned down and whispered, "I'll need Daard's help for this."

The woman must have heard her, because soon, Daard was called into the ring to join us. When he arrived, he gave Missy a reassuring smile, his calm presence helping her relax. Together, they answered questions, explaining our training journey, the dedication it took, and the special bond we'd built over the years. As they spoke, Missy's confidence grew, her voice steady and proud as she shared our story.

The crowd clapped once more when they were done, and Missy's face beamed with happiness. I could feel her pride, and I knew I'd done my part to help her succeed. As we left the ring, I gave her a final nuzzle, and she patted my head, whispering, "Thank you, Rex. You were amazing." And in that moment, surrounded by her family and with the applause still ringing in our ears, I knew we'd achieved something truly special together.

In the weeks after our big moment at Crufts, things settled back to a calm routine at home. But soon, Missy discovered something surprising—Shaarly and his wife had been keeping a little secret. They'd been sneaking off to Latin American dance classes, learning all kinds of fancy moves, and now they were going to be part of a local dance display to promote their group. I could tell from the sparkle in Missy's eyes that she was as surprised as the rest of us. Daard, Moomy, and the whole family were invited to watch, and the excitement around the house started building all over again.

On the night of the performance, Missy took a chance and decided to bring me along. She slipped on my yellow therapy tabard, and I could tell something was up. She was unusually quiet as we walked up to the entrance of the dance hall, keeping a firm hold on my lead. Just as we got to the doors, a man with a serious face stopped us, pointing to me.

"Sorry, no dogs allowed," he said, his voice firm.

Missy hesitated for a split second, then looked the man in the eye and said, "He's my emotional support dog, and I really need him here." She pointed to my yellow tabard. "He's trained to be calm, and he won't disturb anyone."

I could tell she meant it, in a way. She was nervous and clutching my lead tightly, her knuckles turning a little pale. I leaned against her leg to show her I was right there with her.

The man looked at my tabard, then back at Missy, and after a brief pause, he nodded and waved us through. Missy took a deep breath and smiled, giving me a quick pat on the head. Daard, who'd been watching from nearby, chuckled as we passed. "Stretching the truth just a little there, Missi?" he whispered with a grin. But he didn't seem upset—in fact, he looked more amused than anything else. And I was just happy to be by her side.

Chapter 14

The Dance Performance

Inside, the room was packed with people, all waiting eagerly for the performance to start. The lights dimmed, and I sat quietly beside Missi, sensing her anticipation. She was excited to see Shaarly perform, her eyes scanning the stage.

Soon, the music began, and Shaarly and his wife stepped out onto the floor, along with other dancers. They looked like they'd been practising for ages—moving gracefully, their steps perfectly timed to the beat. The music was lively, and Shaarly had a smile on his face, showing a side of him I hadn't seen before. Everyone watched in admiration, and every so often, Missy would glance down at me, her hand resting on my shoulder as if I was helping her soak it all in.

I stayed calm, knowing that Missy needed me to be steady and quiet in the crowd. I wasn't used to loud music or flashing lights, but being there by her side made it easier to relax. Now and then, Daad or Moomy would look over at us, smiling at Missi's determination to have me there.

After the Performance

When the dancing was over, the applause filled the hall. Shaarly and his wife took a bow, and Missy clapped with enthusiasm, her face beaming with pride. As we made our way to meet them afterwards, people in the crowd noticed me and stopped to ask about my role as a therapy dog. Missy was happy to explain, sharing stories about our visits and how much joy I'd brought to her and others. The room was filled with friendly faces, and I felt proud to be by her side.

As we finally made our way outside, Daad shook his head, chuckling to himself. "Missi, I'm not sure you'll get away with that everywhere," he said, his eyes twinkling with amusement. "But I have to admit, Rex handled it perfectly."

Missy gave me a big hug, her smile full of pride. "I couldn't have done it without him," she said simply, patting my head as we walked together, surrounded by family.

And as we left, I felt that same quiet pride I always did after one of our visits. We'd gone somewhere new, been there for each other, and shared a joyful moment with our family. It was another memory added to the many we'd made together, and I couldn't have been happier.

Back in my human self, to give some context: After all the amazing experiences Missy had with Rex, she found herself drawn more and more to the idea of training dogs as a career. Training Rex, preparing for events, therapy visits, and even our trip to Crufts had sparked something in her—a real passion for understanding dogs and helping them learn. She wanted to share the same sense of accomplishment she'd felt with Rex with others.

So, she started researching, looking for courses online. She wanted something reputable and well-recognised, something that would help her learn not only the basics but also the advanced techniques needed to help dogs and their owners build positive, lasting bonds. After a lot of searching and comparing, she found what looked like the perfect option: the British Institute of Professional Dog Trainers (BIPDT).

The course was a little pricey, but after thinking it over, she decided the investment would be worth it if it helped her build a career out of what she loved. Plus, she thought, the skills she would gain could be applied to her work with Rex and other therapy dogs as well. With a mix of excitement and determination, she signed up for the first course.

As she filled out the application, Missy imagined all the possibilities ahead—training therapy dogs like Rex, helping other young handlers gain confidence, and maybe even teaching people of all ages to connect more deeply with their pets. This wasn't just another hobby; it felt like the beginning of something meaningful, something that could turn her passion into a lifelong path.

And with her course booked, Missy felt ready to take her next big step—knowing that, as always, Rex would be right there by her side, her loyal partner in every adventure ahead.

After reviewing the details carefully, Missy saw that this course would be a 7-day intensive training program held in Shropshire. It was no ordinary course—she'd be staying at the college the entire week, living on-site with her dog. The idea of fully immersing herself in this learning experience alongside other aspiring trainers and their dogs was thrilling but also a bit nerve-wracking. She'd never been away for so long on her own, let alone with such a big goal in mind.

Missy imagined the week ahead: working hands-on with Rex every day, learning techniques directly from experienced instructors, and bonding with other dog handlers who shared her passion. Each day would be packed with sessions on advanced training methods, behaviour analysis, and practical exercises. It wouldn't be easy, but she was ready for the challenge.

Staying with Rex would give them both a chance to grow even closer as a team, and Missy felt sure that his calm and steady presence would be a comfort during the intense days of learning. As she prepared for the journey, she could feel her excitement growing. This course was her first step into the world of professional dog training—a place where her love for dogs and her desire to help others could truly flourish.

After what felt like the longest drive ever, we finally pulled up to a place unlike anywhere we'd been before. There were big buildings everywhere, way bigger than the ones at Crufts or the therapy visits. I could feel Missi's hand shaking slightly on my head, her nerves showing through. I looked up at her, giving a reassuring nuzzle to remind her I was here, but she was too focused on the big new world around us to notice.

As we climbed out of the car, a man with a stern face approached us. His expression was serious, but his voice was calm as he "barked" some instructions to Missi, showing us where we needed to go. Missy nodded quickly, following his directions, and we slowly made our way to one of the large buildings where everyone else seemed to be headed.

Inside, we found a big room full of seats for hoomans, each one filled with people who, like Missi, looked a bit anxious and excited. And there were dogs—lots of dogs—all sitting with their hoomans, looking around as confused as I was. Some of the hoomans at the front were barking in the room, using calm, commanding voices as if they were showing the others something important.

I glanced around at the other dogs, catching the curious, wide-eyed stares of a German Shepherd, a fluffy spaniel, and even a big Rottweiler who seemed just as puzzled as I was. We all sat quietly, trying to understand what this new place was about.

Missy leaned down to pat my head, her fingers gently scratching behind my ears. I could feel her starting to relax a little. I knew this was all very new and confusing, but just like at Crufts, we'd figure it out together.

The week started with all of us divided into smaller groups with other handlers and dogs. Each group was led by a hooman who seemed to know exactly what they were doing. The hooman in our group was friendly and had a calm, steady way of barking commands, which seemed to make everyone relax. His dog, however, was a bit... distant. Every time I tried to give him a polite sniff hello, he'd just back away, looking at me like he had better things to do. So, I figured I'd let him be for now. After all, this was a new place, and we had plenty of time.

Missi, I could tell, was in a whirlwind of emotions. Sometimes I'd catch her laughing quietly, especially when all the hoomans started "bonding," as they called it. They'd stand around in groups, talking and sharing stories, and she'd laugh softly as they tried to get her to join in. She was the youngest there, and I could sense her nerves, but over the days, it seemed like everyone began to respect her more and more. I could tell that gave her comfort and confidence, knowing she was being seen as an equal among these hoomans who were mostly much older.

The week was tough, though. Missy was up late every night, studying hard, reading through pages of information, and practising techniques she wanted to perfect. By day, she showed just how much she'd learned, her focus unwavering, even when she was tired. We'd both fall into bed at night, ready for sleep but knowing there'd be another busy day ahead.

After several days—or what I call "several sleeps"—there was a big gathering one evening where all the hoomans sat together at a long table to eat. At the far end of the room was another table where all the head barkers sat. I had to wait in our room, and even though I tried to be patient, it felt like forever. I could tell something important was happening, but I wasn't quite sure what.

Finally, just as I was about to doze off, the door opened, and there was Missi, bursting through with the biggest smile I'd ever seen. Her eyes sparkled, and she was holding something bright in her hand, waving it around as she rushed over to me. She knelt and wrapped her arms around me, her face pressed into my fur as I felt a few happy tears drop onto my coat. I wagged my tail gently, happy to feel her happiness even if I didn't understand exactly what was going on.

She quickly clipped my lead on, and we went for a long walk outside, the cool air filling my nose with the fresh scents of night. As we walked, I could feel her emotions flowing through her. Sometimes she was laughing, sometimes crying softly, and at other times, she was skipping along with pure joy. I stayed close, feeling her excitement ripple through me. I didn't need to know all the details to understand this was a special moment—something she'd worked so hard for, something that had meant everything to her.

And as she whispered "Thank you, Rex" into my ear, I felt a surge of pride. We'd done this together and seeing her so happy was the best reward I could ever ask for. It was the proudest I'd ever felt to be by her side.

Now back home after her week in Shropshire, Missy felt more determined than ever to turn her passion into a career. Armed with her new knowledge and qualifications, she wasted no time and decided to set up her training school. She called it *Paws Obedience Training School* and started with just a few clients—mostly people she'd met through her work with Rex or neighbours curious about her new venture.

At first, things were slow, but word quickly spread about her training methods and the connection she had with both dogs and their owners. People appreciated her calm approach and her ability to make training enjoyable, focusing on building trust and clear communication between hoomans and their dogs. Soon enough, Missi's classes began to fill up, and she found herself with over ten people in each lesson. To keep the classes small and personal, she added more sessions throughout the week, holding classes in different community halls around town.

Her reputation continued to grow as clients shared stories of their progress, and the demand kept increasing. The three sessions a week were full, each one with dogs of all breeds, ages, and personalities, and Missi's confidence as a trainer blossomed. She managed to keep the groups small enough to give each handler and dog personalised attention, making sure everyone felt they got valuable, quality time in her classes.

Paws Obedience Training School quickly became a local favourite, and with her steady presence, dedication, and love for dogs, Missy had truly found her calling.

In every class, Rex was right there by Missi's side, his yellow therapy tabard a familiar sight to the regulars at Paws Obedience Training School. He would trot out into the centre when Missy needed to demonstrate a skill, from basic commands to the more advanced techniques she'd learned at her course. Even though he moved a bit slower now and had to pace himself, his calm, steady presence made him the perfect example for her students. For Rex, it was pure joy, a chance to show off his skills while spending time with Missy and being part of her growing school.

Switching back to being the human to explain Missi's next big step: Inspired by how much she'd loved her work with the Good Citizen Award Scheme when she was training with

Rex, Missy decided to take it a step further. She applied to the Kennel Club to become an official instructor for the Good Citizen Dog Training Scheme, hoping to add this nationally recognised program to her training school's offerings. She knew it would give her students an opportunity to set solid goals and earn achievements with their dogs, something that had meant so much to her and Rex.

After a few weeks of waiting, the response finally arrived. The Kennel Club approved her application, sending a large package full of forms, course materials, and information on the requirements for each level of the award scheme. The whole family was thrilled, celebrating yet another of Missi's accomplishments. Daad, Moomy, and Missy were all buzzing with excitement as they looked through the materials, and even Rex seemed to pick up on the happy energy filling the room.

A few days later, Shaarly and his wife stopped by with their young child, who had spent time with Rex before and was thrilled to see him again. They had come to congratulate both Missy and Rex, knowing how much they had achieved together and how inspiring their story was. The little one toddled over to

Rex, gently patting his fur with that wide-eyed excitement only young children have.

Missy watched the scene unfold, her heart full as she saw her beloved partner, Rex, patiently sitting with the child who reached out to him with so much love. The bond between Rex and the family—old and new—was a testament to the journey they'd all taken together, a journey that had brought so much joy, growth, and hope to all of them. And as Missy looked at Rex, she knew there were still many more adventures to come.

The excitement in the house was electric. I could feel it the moment I saw everyone getting ready, and I knew something special was about to happen. Missy was bustling around, talking excitedly with Moomy and Daad. Then Shaarly and his partner arrived, looking all dressed up and glowing with happiness. I watched everyone, my tail wagging as I tried to understand what was going on.

Then, Missy came over to me with my yellow Pets As Therapy cover. I knew this meant I was going somewhere, and I stood still as she put it on, ready for whatever was ahead. "We're going to see Shaarly dance again, Rex," she whispered, giving me a gentle pat. "And you're coming with us."

I didn't fully understand what a dance competition was, but I remembered the last time we saw Shaarly perform. The music, the crowd, and the excitement of it all stayed with me. Missy and the whole family seemed just as thrilled as I was, and soon we were off, piled into the big moving box and on our way.

Arriving at the Competition

When we got to the hall, I could hear the music even from outside. There were so many new scents in the air—perfume, flowers, polished floors, and the faint smell of snacks being prepared somewhere nearby. Missy kept a steady hand on my lead as we made our way to the entrance.

Once again, we were stopped at the door. A lady looked down at me, her eyebrows raising slightly. "No dogs allowed," she said firmly, glancing at my yellow cover.

Missy took a deep breath and gave her a confident smile. "He's my emotional support dog. He'll stay calm, and he helps me feel more comfortable in crowded places," she said, just like she'd done before. I stayed perfectly still, looking up at the lady with my best calm expression.

After a moment's hesitation, she nodded. "Alright then. But keep him close," she said, letting us through. Missy gave my head a quick pat, and I could feel her relief.

As we walked inside, I could tell Daad had noticed what happened. He gave Missy a small grin, a twinkle in his eye. "Stretching the truth a little again, Missi?" he teased, but he didn't seem upset—in fact, he seemed a little proud of her confidence.

Chapter 15

The Competition Begins

We found our seats near the front, and Missy settled me beside her, keeping a gentle hand on my lead. The lights dimmed, and soon, the music began. I stayed calm as the sounds filled the room, watching as people stepped onto the floor, their movements graceful and lively. The crowd clapped and cheered, creating an energy that seemed to fill the whole space.

Then, I saw Shaarly and his partner step out onto the floor. They both looked amazing and even I could sense the pride and confidence they carried. The music changed, and they started to move together in perfect rhythm, gliding, spinning, and stepping in a mesmerizing way. Missy leaned forward, her eyes fixed on them, her face glowing with pride.

People around us clapped and cheered, and Missy joined in, clapping softly while keeping a steady hand on my lead. I sat calmly, letting the joyful energy in the room wash over me. Now and then, I'd glance up at Missi, happy to see her so at ease and so proud of her brother.

A Proud Moment

When Shaarly and his partner finished their dance, the crowd erupted into applause, filling the room with the loudest sounds I'd ever heard. I felt Missi's hand tighten on my lead as she joined in, her excitement radiating through her. Shaarly and his partner took their bows, their faces bright with joy, and Missi's eyes sparkled with pride.

After the competition, we went to meet them. Shaarly grinned when he saw us, and he knelt to scratch behind my ears. "Did you see me out there, Rex?" he said with a laugh. I wagged my tail, giving him a gentle nuzzle, letting him know I'd been watching the whole time.

Missy hugged him, congratulating him and his partner with that same joy she always had when we celebrated something as a family. And even though I wasn't sure what all the clapping, lights, and music meant,

I could tell it was something big—something that brought us all closer together.

As we made our way back home, I felt proud, knowing that I'd been part of this special day with my family once again. It didn't matter if I understood everything; being there with them was all that mattered.

Over many, many sleeps, my days settled into a familiar rhythm, filled with special visits to the hoomans who needed me most. Each visit brought something a little different, and I'd learned to tell, from the sounds and scents, just who I was going to be meeting that day.

Visits to the Older Hoomans

The visits to the older hoomans were always calm and gentle. We'd walk through long hallways with that particular scent I'd come to know, a mix of warm blankets, tea, and sometimes a hint of flowers. When we entered the big room where the older hoomans sat, many of them would turn their heads, their eyes lighting up when they saw me. Their faces, often creased with age, would soften into warm smiles as I approached.

Some of them would reach out slowly, their hands gentle and careful, stroking my head or patting my back. They would talk to me in soft, soothing voices, telling me stories I couldn't understand but felt honoured to hear. Sometimes, they'd call me their "good boy" and tell me about the dogs they had loved before. I could feel the warmth in their words, and it made me want to stay by their side, giving them as much comfort as I could.

Every so often, one of the older hoomans would have tears in their eyes, and I'd sit quietly by them, resting my head in their lap. They'd pat me softly, their fingers stroking my fur as they spoke gently, often whispering things I couldn't quite catch. I knew that just by being there, I was helping in a way that words couldn't.

Visits to the Young Hoomans

Then there were the visits to the young hoomans— the children, who always brought such lively energy.

When I walked into a classroom or therapy session, their excitement was infectious. Some would squeal with delight, while others would reach out immediately, eager to pet me and tell me all about their day.

The young hoomans would sit in a circle, each one waiting for their turn to read to me. They'd open their books, their voices sometimes shaky but always determined. I'd sit patiently, listening as they read their stories aloud, glancing up at me now and then to see if I was paying attention. When they stumbled over a word, I'd wag my tail gently, encouraging them to keep going.

Some children would come close but stay quiet, their hands resting on my fur without saying much. I could sense their shyness, so I'd nudge them gently or rest my head in their lap, letting them know I was there for them, too. By the end of each visit, I felt as though I'd made new friends, young hoomans who looked at me with wide, trusting eyes.

Visits to the Not-So-Well Hoomans

The visits to the not-so-well hoomans were different. These were the hoomans who were in the big building with the strong, strange smells and the beeping noises—the hospital. These hoomans often looked tired, sometimes lying in beds with tubes and wires connected to them. Their rooms were quieter, the lighting soft, and I'd enter carefully, staying close to Missy as we approached each bed.

Some of the not-so-well hoomans would smile weakly when they saw me, their eyes brightening for a moment as I came close. They'd reach out, their hands sometimes shaky, and I'd sit still, letting them pet me and feel the warmth of my fur. A gentle pat, a soft stroke, and I'd feel their spirits lift just a little. Missy would often talk softly to them, sharing stories of our visits, and I'd stay close, knowing that my presence was bringing them comfort.

Other times, the not-so-well hoomans were children, their small bodies tucked into big hospital beds.

Their voices were soft, sometimes tired, but they'd smile when I came over, whispering my name as they reached out to touch me. I'd wag my tail just a little, wanting to bring a bit of joy to their day, and sometimes, they'd ask me to lie down beside them, where they could rest their small hands on my fur, but Missy said I could stay by the bed but not on it.

Together in Every Visit

Through all these visits—whether to the older hoomans, the young hoomans, or the not-so-well ones—Missy was always by my side, her voice calm and steady as she guided me. Her gentle words reassured me, and I could feel her pride in each interaction. She knew, just as I did that our visits made a difference.

Over many sleeps, these moments became our routine, our purpose. Each visit was filled with small gestures of love and comfort, a quiet understanding shared between us and the hoomans we met. It didn't matter that I couldn't understand their words; I could feel the emotions in every pet, every smile, every gentle whisper. And with each goodbye, I knew I had done something meaningful, something good.

I should add that between our visits to the older hoomans, young hoomans, and not-so-well ones. There were days filled with pure joy and rest. Daad and Moomy would take me out for long walks, leading me to the big green areas where I could stretch my legs, breathe in the fresh air, and feel like a young pup again, if only for a little while.

These green places were vast, filled with soft grass, tall trees, and so many new scents that I could have spent hours just sniffing around. I loved feeling the cool ground beneath my paws as I trotted along beside them, keeping my nose low, catching the scent trails of other dogs, maybe a squirrel or two, and the faint, earthy smell of fresh dew on the grass.

Sometimes, Shaarly, his wife, and their little one would join us. They'd bring along snacks, and the little one, who always looked at me with those big, wide eyes, would laugh as I tried to keep up. I'd do my best to run and play, wagging my tail and trying to keep pace with everyone, feeling the happy, playful energy that buzzed around them. I'd chase after Shaarly, follow the little one as they shuffled along, and let the whole family dote on me with gentle pats and scratches behind the ears.

But lately, I'd found myself getting tired more quickly. Even if my heart wanted to run forever, my legs seemed to grow heavy sooner than they used to, and I'd have to slow down and catch my breath. Moomy and Daad seemed to notice, giving me a little break by sitting down on a bench or the grass beside me, stroking my back as I panted, letting me rest.

When it was time to head home, I'd feel a gentle nudge of relief. I'd enjoyed the time out, the running and playing, but as we turned back toward the house, I'd often feel an anxious pull to get home and rest. My soft bed was waiting for me, a cosy place where I could relax and feel safe, surrounded by the comforting scents of my family.

Each outing reminded me of how lucky I was—to have these people who loved me, who understood when I needed a break, and who were patient with me as I grew older. They always seemed to know that I needed these moments of joy but also the peace of home afterwards. And as I drifted off to sleep after a long, fulfilling day, I knew that no matter what, they'd always be there for me, just as I had been for them.

One bright morning, Missy and I set out together for a special visit to a nearby Dog Training Club. She had been called to assess dogs for the Bronze, Silver, and Gold Good Citizen Awards, a role she had worked hard to achieve. I could sense her excitement mixed with a hint of nerves, but mostly, she seemed eager and proud to put her skills to use and help other hoomans and their dogs reach their goals.

I trotted beside her. Although I was a bit slower these days, I knew my presence calmed Missi, and I was glad to be there for her. When we arrived at the club, a group of dogs and their handlers were gathered outside, each one waiting with that mix of anticipation and determination I'd seen so many times during my training.

We entered the building, which was filled with the smells of other dogs, treats, and the faint, earthy scent of well-worn training mats. Missi's calm confidence showed as she introduced herself to the club members and began explaining how the day's tests would unfold. She outlined the requirements for each level—Bronze, Silver, and Gold—and I could see how much her words meant to everyone. They all looked at her with respect, listening intently to her guidance.

First came the Bronze level, which was for dogs just beginning their journey with obedience and manners. Missy watched as each dog and handler demonstrated skills like walking calmly on a lead, sitting, staying, and responding to basic commands. I sat beside her, observing quietly as the dogs worked through the exercises. Some struggled a little, their tails wagging anxiously, but Missy offered encouragement and gentle feedback, guiding each handler on how they could improve.

Next, it was time for the silver level. This group had a bit more experience, and I could see the dedication in both the hoomans and their dogs. Missy assessed each dog carefully, watching as they tackled the more advanced tasks like longer stays, walking on a loose lead around distractions, and coming when called.

Finally, it was time for the Gold level—the highest achievement in the Good Citizen scheme. The dogs attempting this test were truly impressive, showing off their skills with calm confidence. Missy watched closely as each team demonstrated everything from advanced recalls and controlled waits to polite greetings with strangers. She was thorough and fair in her assessments, giving each handler feedback and advice. Some dogs passed with flying colours, while others received encouragement to keep working toward their goal.

Throughout the day, I noticed the hoomans giving me warm smiles and soft pats as they passed by. They'd heard about my role as Missy's therapy dog and her inspiration for becoming a trainer. I felt proud to see her sharing her knowledge with others, helping them reach the same milestones we had once celebrated together.

When the last dog had finished the Gold test, Missy called everyone together, giving a final summary and congratulating those who had passed. She offered kind words to those who would need to come back and try again, her voice filled with encouragement and support.

As we headed home, Missy leaned down to scratch behind my ears, her face beaming with pride. "Thanks for being there with me, Rex," she said softly. "You're always my good boy."

<u>Rex's Thought</u> – *Ah, yes! They've found the spot. Right there. Don't stop now! These hoomans really do know how to make me feel like royalty.*

As I settled into my spot in the big box, I knew that today had been just as much a testament to our journey together as it was to her growth as a trainer. We had come full circle, and I was grateful to have been by her side for every step.

One night, the world outside seemed to come alive with loud, frightening noises. I'd heard these sounds before, but tonight, they were worse than ever. Some bangs shook the ground, shrill whizzing sounds that shot through the air, and crackling bursts that exploded into the sky. I'd heard Missy call them "fryerwoorks" before, but it had never sounded this intense. Each bang felt louder, sharper, and closer than ever, and I was more frightened than I'd ever been in my life.

The first few explosions sent me skittering across the floor, my heart pounding as I looked for somewhere safe to hide. I couldn't escape the noises—they were everywhere. Every time I tried to settle, another burst would go off, making my ears twitch and my body shake. I felt so small and helpless like there was no way to get away from the noise.

Missy noticed right away. She looked at me with that calm, understanding gaze she always had when she knew something was wrong. "It's okay, Rex," she said softly, her voice calm and steady, even though my whole world was crumbling with every bang. She told me, again, that it was something called "fryerwoorks" and that this noise was only temporary. But as much as I wanted to believe her, it was hard to feel safe with such loud, unfamiliar sounds.

I went over to her, looking up at her with wide eyes, my whole body shaking. She didn't force me to come closer or make me do anything, but she lowered herself to the ground beside me, staying close without crowding me. Her presence was warm and steady, like an anchor in the middle of the storm. She reached out slowly, her hand resting gently on my back. I could feel the warmth of her touch, and it was comforting, even if my heart was still racing.

"Rex, it's okay to be scared," she murmured, her voice soft and steady as if she were trying to fill the space between the bangs with calmness. "I'll stay right here. I won't go anywhere." She didn't try to hush me or stop my shaking—she just stayed beside me, letting me know she was there.

Slowly, I edged a little closer, laying my head on her knee. She started to rub my ears in that way she knew

I loved, her touch calm and comforting. Even as another loud burst went off outside, her hand stayed steady, letting me know that she wasn't going to leave, no matter how scary the night got.

As the noises continued, I still jumped and trembled with each bang. But knowing that Missy was there, her calm presence beside me, made it a little easier to bear. I understood, somehow, that it was okay to be frightened—that I didn't have to pretend to be brave. She wasn't going to leave my side; she'd stay right here until it was over.

The night dragged on, with bangs and whizzing sounds that seemed to stretch for hours. But Missy stayed with me through every one of them, whispering reassuring words and keeping her hand on my back, never pulling away. And even though I was scared, even though my body shook with every noise, I trusted her. I knew that as long as she was beside me, I'd make it through the night.

By the time the noises finally stopped, and the world grew quiet again, I was exhausted. Missy's hand stayed on me, and she whispered softly, "See? It's over now. You did so well, Rex."

As the quiet settled in around us, I lay down beside her, feeling my body finally relax. I still didn't understand what "fryerwoorks" were or why they had to be so loud, but I did understand one thing—Missy was my safe place, and as long as I had her, I knew I could face even the scariest nights.

Not long after that scary night with the fireworks, something unsettling started happening again. My balance, which had been mostly steady for a while, began to feel off once more. It was as though the ground was shifting under me, and sometimes, my paws couldn't take me exactly where I wanted to go. I'd stumble or sway a little, even when I was just standing still, and I could see the worry in Missy's eyes whenever I'd wobble.

Before long, I found myself back in the place I'd come to think of as the place of stings and strange smells.

The familiar scent of medicine and antiseptic filled the air, and my nerves stirred up as we walked through the door. But I stayed calm, knowing that Missy and Mr. Richardson were right there with me. They would not let anything bad happen.

We were greeted by a hooman I hadn't met before. He had a gentle face and kind eyes, and I could sense his patience as he knelt to look me over, his hands moving gently and carefully. He spoke in a calm voice, which helped me relax a little, even though I still felt unsteady. He didn't sting me or poke me with anything sharp—just a gentle touch here and there, watching my movements carefully as I sat and tried to stay steady.

As he examined me, I watched Mr. Richardson's face. He was listening closely, nodding every so often as the hooman talked to him in soft, steady tones. I couldn't understand their words, but I knew they were talking about me. The hooman glanced over at me with a kind smile before turning back to Mr. Richardson, his voice low and calm as he continued explaining something.

I stayed still, feeling a bit tired and dizzy, but there was something comforting about the way the hooman spoke and moved. He didn't rush, didn't make me feel scared—he just kept that steady, soothing presence, which made it easier to stay calm, even in this place of strange smells and past stings.

After a long time, the hooman finished talking to Mr. Richardson and leaned down to pat my head gently. I wasn't sure what all of this meant, but I knew they were doing their best to help me feel better, and I trusted them to make the right choices. As we made our way back home, Mr. Richardson gave me a reassuring pat, and Missy gently scratched my ears, whispering that I'd done a good job.

And as I lay down in the quiet of home, I felt their love surrounding me, a reminder that, no matter what, I wasn't alone in this. They'd be there every step of the way, just as they always had been.

I hadn't been asleep for long when I heard the familiar sounds of Shaarly's voice and the soft voice of his wife as they entered the house. Soon enough, I could smell the comforting scents of everyone—Mr. and Mrs. Richardson, Missy, and Shaarly's little one, who shuffled in with a happy giggle. One by one, they gathered around me, settling down in a circle as if to share a quiet, special moment.

I lifted my head, my heartwarming as I looked around at all of them. Something was calming about having everyone here, surrounding me with love and familiar faces. I felt a deep sense of peace as they each reached out, some patting my back, others gently rubbing my ears or scratching behind my neck in the way they knew I loved. I leaned into their touches, feeling the warmth of each hand as it rested gently on me.

Missy sat right by my side, her hand resting on my head, and I could feel her gentle, steady breathing as she looked down at me. Her eyes were shining, wet with tears that she tried to blink away, but she still managed a brave smile. I knew she was trying to be strong, trying to comfort me, even though her heart felt heavy. I gave her a gentle nuzzle, letting her know I was here, that I felt her love, and that it was okay.

Everyone was quiet, their faces soft with smiles and eyes full of memories, each one holding onto a piece of our time together. I could feel the love in that room, filling the space around me like a warm blanket. It was as if each of them was silently telling me, "Thank you for being here, for everything you've given us." And I wanted them to know how much they meant to me, too.

For a while, we just stayed there, all together, with no words needed. The quiet was filled with love, peace, and gratitude. And in that moment, I felt truly blessed, surrounded by the family who had given me a life filled with joy, adventure, and unconditional love.

That night, as I curled up on my bed, I felt a gentle wave of dizziness pass over me, but it was softened by the warmth surrounding me. I could still feel the touch of each hand and the quiet love from everyone who had gathered around me, filling my heart with a deep sense of peace.

<u>Rex's Thought</u> - *This spot by the warm fire is my favourite. My family's all here, and the world feels quiet. I think this is what it means to be happy.*

I took a long, slow breath, letting myself sink into the comforting softness of my bed, feeling safe and cared for. The scents of home—the familiar smells of my family and all the places we'd been together—lingered around me, wrapping me in memories of happy times. I thought about all the moments we'd shared, the walks, the visits, the adventures, and the quiet times spent just being together.

As my eyes grew heavy, I felt gratitude swell inside me. What a family I had—people who loved me without question and who filled my days with purpose, laughter, and calm. And what a life I'd been given. A life where I'd been part of so many hearts, where I'd felt love in every scratch behind the ears, every gentle word, every shared moment.

With a final, contented sigh, I drifted off, feeling blessed, warm, and happy. Whatever lay ahead, I knew I'd been given a life that was full and rich in ways that truly mattered. And as sleep took me, I felt nothing but peace.

Rex drifted into a peaceful sleep that night, surrounded by the warmth and love of his family. He never woke up, passing away quietly at the age of 15, with the same gentle spirit that had filled every moment of his life.

As the morning light crept into the house, the family found him lying peacefully, a soft look of contentment on his face. Though their hearts ached, they took comfort in knowing he had passed away gently, wrapped in the love he had given them every day of his life.

For Missy, the loss was deeply felt; Rex had been her partner, her loyal companion through every milestone. She had grown up with him by her side, learning life's lessons, building her dreams, and finding her path. He had been so much more than a pet—he was her confidant, her guide, and her best friend. She was proud to have been there for him in his final years, just as he had been there for her all along.

Shaarly, too, mourned the loss of his "brother." Rex had been a constant presence in his life, there for every laugh, every family gathering, every moment that truly mattered. Shaarly and his wife shared stories of Rex with their young child, ensuring that the warmth and joy he brought to their lives would be remembered and passed down, even after he was gone.

Mr. and Mrs. Richardson felt the weight of his absence deeply, remembering the day they first brought him home and the love he had brought to their family. They had given him a home, but he had given them a lifetime of loyalty and companionship, enriching their lives in ways they hadn't anticipated. He had been a part of their family, not only as a dog but as a cherished member whose spirit had filled their home with joy and warmth.

Though Rex was gone, he left behind a legacy of love, trust, and memories that would live in their hearts forever. His gentle spirit had touched everyone he met—from the older hoomans and young children to the strangers he brought comfort to during his visits. His life had been full, blessed with purpose, companionship, and the quiet satisfaction of having been deeply loved.

And in the years to come, his family would carry his memory forward, remembering him not only as a beloved pet but as a friend, a teacher, and a cherished part of their lives. Rex's journey had come to an end, but the love he had shared remained, woven into the hearts of those who had been lucky enough to be part of his story.

Printed in Great Britain
by Amazon